HOLY, HOLY, HOLY

PROCLAIMING *the* PERFECTIONS *of* GOD

Thabiti Anyabwile, Alistair Begg, D.A. Carson

Sinclair B. Ferguson, W. Robert Godfrey, Steven J. Lawson

R.C. Sproul, R.C. Sproul Jr., Derek W.H. Thomas

℞

Reformation Trust

PUBLISHING

A DIVISION OF LIGONIER MINISTRIES · ORLANDO, FLORIDA

Holy, Holy, Holy: Proclaiming the Perfections of God

© 2010 by Ligonier Ministries

Published by Reformation Trust
a division of Ligonier Ministries
400 Technology Park, Lake Mary, FL 32746
www.ligonier.org   www.reformationtrust.com

Printed in Harrisonburg, Virginia
RR Donnelly and Sons
May 2010
First Edition

Cover design: Metaleap Design
Illustration: Olaf Hajek
Interior design and typeset: Katherine Lloyd, The DESK

Unless otherwise noted, Scripture quotations are from The Holy Bible, English Standard Version®, copyright © 2001 by Crossway Bibles, a publishing ministry of Good News Publishers. Used by permission. All rights reserved.

Unless otherwise indicated, all Scripture quotations in Chapter 7, and all Scripture quotations elsewhere marked NIV, are from the HOLY BIBLE, NEW INTERNATIONAL VERSION®. NIV®. Copyright © 1973, 1978, 1984 by International Bible Society. Used by permission of Zondervan. All rights reserved.

Unless otherwise indicated, all Scripture quotations in Chapter 10, and all Scripture quotations elsewhere marked NKJV, are from the New King James Version®. Copyright © 1982 by Thomas Nelson. Used by permission. All rights reserved.

Scripture quotations marked NASB are from the New American Standard Bible®, copyright © 1960, 1962, 1963, 1968, 1971, 1972, 1973, 1975, 1995 by The Lockman Foundation. Used by permission. (www.Lockman.org)

Scripture quotations marked KJV are from The Holy Bible, King James Version.

Library of Congress Cataloging-in-Publication Data

Holy, holy, holy : proclaiming the perfections of God / Thabiti Anyabwile ... [et al.].
    p. cm.
  Includes bibliographical references and index.
  ISBN 978-1-56769-205-1
  1. God (Christianity) 2. God (Christianity)--Holiness. I. Anyabwile, Thabiti M., 1970-
  BT103.H67 2010
  231'.4--dc22
                                                          2010005919

CONTENTS

PREFACE

It has now been twenty-five years since the first edition of my book *The Holiness of God* was published. It has been more years than that since I first taught on this subject. And it has been more years still since the subject of God's holiness first gripped my attention with a force that has never diminished.

I was first exposed to the great titans of church history when I entered college. There I encountered men such as Athanasius, Anselm, Thomas Aquinas, Martin Luther, John Calvin, Jonathan Edwards, Charles Spurgeon, and others of that stripe. I soon saw that these men differed on some points of theology. Clearly they had different personalities, gifts, and talents. But I discovered one strand that ran through the works of all these men—they were intoxicated by a profound sense of the majesty and of the holiness of God.

In the very beginning of his greatest work, the *Institutes of the Christian Religion*, Calvin remarks on our detrimental tendency as human beings to keep our gaze fixed on this terrestrial plane: "As long as we do not look beyond the earth, being quite content with our own righteousness, wisdom, and virtue, we flatter ourselves most sweetly, and fancy ourselves all but demigods." However, he added, if we just once lift our gaze to heaven and contemplate what kind of being God is, we gain a very different perspective on ourselves: "What wonderfully impressed us under the name of wisdom will stink in its very foolishness."[1] By raising our gaze, we come to understand the universal testimony of holy men in the pages of sacred Scripture, who, having had a momentary glimpse of the character of God, were reduced to trembling in dust and in ashes.

I believe the church desperately needs this perspective like never before. That is why I continue to preach, teach, and proclaim the holiness of God, and why I will continue to do so, God willing, until my final breath.

This book is a reflection of that commitment. These chapters originated as lectures at the 2009 Ligonier Ministries National Conference in Orlando. The theme of that conference was "The Holiness of God." As at similarly themed Ligonier conferences in the past, the gifted speakers gave the attendees a clearer vision of the God we worship and taught powerfully on the implications of His holiness. I believe those brothers and sisters went away with their gazes lifted to a higher plane.

It is my prayer that this book will lift your gaze as well. May you be revived as you contemplate anew the character of our holy God, leading to an overwhelming passion for Him. Then may you take that passion for His holiness into the church and the world at large, which so needs to see God as He truly is.

—*R. C. Sproul*
Longwood, Florida
January 2010

Note

1 John Calvin, *Institutes of the Christian Religion*, Library of Christian Classics, vols. XX–XXI, ed. John T. McNeill, trans. Ford Lewis Battles (Louisville: Westminster John Knox, 1960), 1.1.2.

CONTRIBUTORS

Thabiti Anyabwile is senior pastor of First Baptist Church in Grand Cayman, Cayman Islands. Rev. Anyabwile is a sought-after conference speaker and is the author of several books, including *The Decline of African American Theology: From Biblical Faith to Cultural Captivity*, *The Faithful Preacher: Recapturing the Vision of Three Pioneering African-American Pastors*, and *What Is a Healthy Church Member?*

Alistair Begg is senior pastor of Parkside Church in Cleveland, Ohio, and can be heard teaching daily on the radio program *Truth for Life*. Dr. Begg has served in pastoral ministry for more than thirty years and has written numerous books, including *The Hand of God*, *Lasting Love*, and *Made for His Pleasure*.

D. A. Carson is research professor of New Testament at Trinity Evangelical Divinity School in Deerfield, Illinois. He is a widely sought-after conference speaker and teacher, and he is known in the church for his excellence in scholarship and passion for the biblical gospel. Dr. Carson has authored more than forty-five books, including *The Gagging of God*, *Scripture and Truth*, and the commentary on *Matthew* in the Expositors' Biblical Commentary series.

Sinclair B. Ferguson is senior minister of the historical First Presbyterian Church in Columbia, South Carolina. He also serves as a professor of systematic theology at Redeemer Theological Seminary in Dallas, Texas, and as a teaching fellow of Ligonier Ministries. He is a trustee of the Banner of Truth Trust publishing house and is a member of the council of the Alliance of Confessing Evangelicals. His many books include *By Grace Alone: How the Grace of God Amazes Me*, *The Holy Spirit*, *Grow in Grace*,

Let's Study Philippians, John Owen on the Christian Life, In Christ Alone: Living the Gospel-Centered Life, and, for children, *The Big Book of Questions & Answers* and *The Big Book of Questions & Answers About Jesus.*

W. Robert Godfrey is president and professor of church history at Westminster Seminary California in Escondido, California. He has taught at many colleges and seminaries, and speaks frequently at Christian conferences across the country. A teaching fellow of Ligonier Ministries and a member of the Council of the Alliance of Confessing Evangelicals, Dr. Godfrey has written several books, including *An Unexpected Journey, Reformation Sketches*, and *Pleasing God in Our Worship.*

Steven J. Lawson is senior pastor of Christ Fellowship Baptist Church in Mobile, Alabama. He serves on the ministerial board for Reformed Theological Seminary and the board of directors for The Master's College and Seminary, and is a teaching fellow of Ligonier Ministries. Dr. Lawson has authored many books, including *Famine in the Land, Foundations of Grace, The Expository Genius of John Calvin*, and *The Unwavering Resolve of Jonathan Edwards.*

R. C. Sproul is recognized throughout the church for his articulate and winsome proclamation of the holiness of God and other essential doctrines of the Christian faith. As the founder and president of Ligonier Ministries, his teaching can be heard on the program *Renewing Your Mind*, which is available on hundreds of radio outlets in the United States and in fifty countries worldwide. Dr. Sproul also serves as the chancellor of the Ligonier Academy of Biblical and Theological Studies and as senior minister of preaching and teaching at Saint Andrew's in Sanford, Florida. He has authored more than seventy books, including *The Holiness of God, The Truth of the Cross, Truths We Confess*, and *The Lightlings.*

R. C. Sproul Jr. serves as a teaching fellow of Ligonier Ministries. He planted Saint Peter Presbyterian Church in Southwest Virginia and is the founder, chairman, and teacher of Highlands Ministries. Dr. Sproul travels extensively as a conference speaker and has written several books, including *Believing God, Tearing Down Strongholds, When You Rise Up, Bound for Glory,* and *Biblical Economics.*

Derek W. H. Thomas is professor of practical and systematic theology at Reformed Theological Seminary in Jackson, Mississippi. He is also the minister of teaching at First Presbyterian Church in Jackson, Mississippi, and editorial director for the Alliance of Confessing Evangelicals. Among Dr. Thomas' many books are *God Strengthens: Ezekiel Properly Explained, Mining for Wisdom,* and *Calvin's Teaching on Job.*

"I AM THE LORD":

THE ONLY GOD

- R. C. Sproul -

As WE BEGIN OUR CONSIDERATION OF THE HOLINESS OF GOD, I would like to examine a brief portion of the book of Isaiah—but it is not from Isaiah 6, from which I have often taught about God's holiness. I want to look instead at Isaiah 45:1–8:

> Thus says the LORD to his anointed, to Cyrus, whose right hand I have grasped, to subdue nations before him and to loose the belts of kings, to open doors before him that gates may not be closed: "I will go before you and level the exalted places. I will break in pieces the doors of bronze and cut through the bars of iron, I will give you the treasures of darkness and the hoards in secret places, that you may know that it is I, the LORD, the God of Israel, who call you by your name. For the sake of my servant Jacob, and Israel my chosen, I call you by your name, I name you, though you do not know me. I am

the LORD, and there is no other, besides me there is no God. I equip you, though you do not know me, that people may know, from the rising of the sun and from the west, that there is none besides me; I am the LORD, and there is no other. I form light and create darkness, I make well-being and create calamity, I am the LORD, who does all these things. Shower, O heavens, from above, and let the clouds rain down righteousness; let the earth open, that salvation and righteousness may bear fruit; and let the earth cause them both to sprout; I the LORD have created it."

This is one of the strangest texts we find anywhere in sacred Scripture. It is a message of divine revelation from God to a man by the name of Cyrus, who was not yet alive when this message was given. At the time of this prophecy, Israel was in the midst of its Babylonian captivity, subjugated by the most powerful empire on the face of the earth. But the message in this text is not addressed to someone from Babylon. It is addressed to a future king of the Persian/Median Empire, who would defeat the Babylonians and ultimately liberate the people of Israel to return to their homeland.

In this passage, God begins by saying that He is speaking "to his anointed, to Cyrus." This verse scandalized the Jewish people, who were astonished that God would call a future Gentile king His "anointed." Nowhere else in Scripture do we find this title used for anyone outside of Israel.

What follows is hardly less astonishing. God says to Cyrus: "Thus says the LORD to Cyrus, whose right hand I have grasped, to subdue nations before him and to loose the belts of kings, to open doors before him that gates may not be closed: 'I will go before you and level the exalted places, I will break in pieces the doors of bronze and cut through the bars of iron, I will give you the treasures of darkness and the hoards in secret places" (vv. 1–3a). In effect, God is saying: "I am the Lord God. I have anointed you and I will go before you. I will give you the power in your armies to lay waste to the strongholds that rule the world right now. I will take your right arm in My right arm. I will break the bars and the bronze shields. I will give you treasures." The list of things God vows to do goes on and on.

Why is God going to do this? He tells Cyrus plainly: "That you may know that it is I, the LORD, the God of Israel, who call you by your name. For the sake of my servant Jacob, and Israel my chosen, I call you by your name, I name you, though you do not know me" (vv. 3b–4). In other words, God says: "I am going to do this, Cyrus, so that you may know who I am, that you may know that I am the Lord God of Israel. But ultimately, this will be not just for your sake, but for the sake of My people, Israel."

John Calvin, the great theologian of the Protestant Reformation, once made a comment that I appreciate: "Let us, I say, allow the Christian to unlock his mind and ears to all the words of God which are addressed to him, provided he do it with this moderation—viz. that whenever the Lord shuts [His] sacred mouth, he also desists from inquiry."[1] That was Calvin's warning against unbridled speculations about the truth of God. But in spite of the influence that warning has had on my life, I can't resist a few speculations here. So with my apologies to the magisterial Reformer John Calvin, I will speculate for a second.

I try to imagine what might have gone through Cyrus' mind when he heard this prophecy for the first time, particularly when we get to the refrain that occurs three times in this chapter: "I am the LORD, and there is no other" (vv. 5a, 6b, 18b). I picture Cyrus hearing these words from this foreign deity, who declares that He is the Lord and that He would like to have a word with Cyrus. Perhaps this Gentile king thought to himself: "Oh, Yahweh . . . yes, he's the Lord of Israel. But I am Cyrus, lord of Persia. So I suppose this deity of Israel would like to have a summit meeting with me so the two of us can sit down and plan my future military campaign."

Maybe that is what Cyrus thought at first. But God didn't allow him to hold that thought, adding, "besides me there is no God" (v. 5b). Does that sound familiar to you? Do you recall hearing anything like that from the pen of Moses? How about Exodus 20:2–3: "I am the LORD your God, who brought you out of the land of Egypt, out of the house of slavery. You shall have no other gods before me"?

These declarations from God to Cyrus affirm the uniqueness of God. In the remainder of this chapter, I want to consider briefly what is unique about the God of the Bible.

Negation and Eminence

The term *holy* has two common references. The first and primary meaning of the term refers to God's otherness—the sense in which He is different from everything else in the created universe. The secondary meaning has to do with His purity, His perfection in righteousness, which we contemplate regularly. In that sense, holiness is a communicable attribute. We know this is so because He says, "Be holy, for I am holy" (Lev. 11:44). But holiness cannot be a communicable attribute in its primary meaning, for it describes something about God that you and I cannot possess in this world or the world to come. It refers to His transcendent, divine nature, the sense in which He is "other" from us.

In systematic theology, when we try to set forth our doctrine of God and detail the attributes of God, we struggle with the limitations of human language. Historically, the theologians of the church have relied on three distinct methods to describe the being and character of God. One of the most common methods, and certainly the favorite one employed by Augustine, is what we call the *via negationis* or *via negativa*—the "way of negation." Quite simply, the way of negation defines something by saying what it is not.

There are several ways we use this method in theology. I'll just mention two of them in passing. First, when we talk about God, we say that He is infinite. That simply means that God is "not finite." We are finite, and to be finite is to have boundaries. There is an edge, a limit, to the sphere in which we live and move and have our being (Acts 17:28). We can be in only one place at a time. But God is not bound by the borders of creatureliness. He is not finite. He is infinite. If we sent spacecraft to probe the deepest places of the universe, no matter how far we went, we would not reach the end of God, because there is no end to a being who is infinite.

A second way in which we use the way of negation to describe God is with the term *immutable*. When we say that God is immutable, we simply mean that He is "not mutable." Nothing defines creaturely existence more directly than the phenomenon of change. Since you picked up this book and began to read it, you have changed. The change may be imperceptible, but if nothing else you are a few minutes older. You have changed, because that is the defining attribute of all created objects and creatures. We live in a world that is constantly changing, but we cannot apply that category to God. He is the same today as He was yesterday and will be tomorrow. One of the most comforting concepts in all of sacred Scripture about the character and the nature of God is that He is immutable—He is not subject to change in His person or in His behavior, that is, His very being.

Another common way we define God is by what is called the *via eminentia*, or "way of eminence." That is, we take normal, human, earthly categories and exalt them to the "nth" degree. For instance, we say that one of the things that we possess as human beings is the capacity to learn, to accumulate knowledge. The contributors to this book are extraordinarily knowledgeable men, but none of them has all knowledge. In other words, we possess elements of science, but God possesses all science or omniscience. In a similar way, we all experience the exercise of power at a creaturely level. Sometimes we are overwhelmed by the manifestation, for example, of the power of nature, such as when earthquakes strike developing countries. We see the power of a tsunami or of a volcanic eruption. The inventions of human power, such as the atomic bomb, boggle the mind. These things are potent in human terms, but they are popguns compared to the power of God, who is all potent or omnipotent. The attribute of omnipotence defines God because only God has all power. He is unique in these ways. "I am the LORD, there is no other."

Affirmations of Uniqueness

In addition to the way of negation and the way of eminence, there is the *via affirmativa*, the "way of affirmation." Again, I'll give you just two illustrations to show how we use this method to define the uniqueness of the holy God. We use it when we say that God, and God alone, is "self-existent" and "eternal." These affirmations take us to the extreme edges of our ability to comprehend who God is.

Of all the theological terms that have been used to describe God in the theological tomes of history, one sends chills up and down my spine so strongly that I can hardly write it on the chalkboard in the classroom without becoming overwhelmed. It is the word *aseity*. If there is any word in the English language that captures the otherness of God, it is the word *aseity*. It means "self-existence." God, and God alone, has the power of being in and of Himself.

When NASA first launched the Hubble Space Telescope, I heard a comment by a famous astrophysicist whose name you would recognize. He said, "I'm excited about the launch of the Hubble Telescope because we are going to learn all kinds of things about the origins of the universe, which exploded into being some twelve to eighteen billion years ago." I was driving when I heard these comments on the radio, and I almost lost it. My hands came right off the wheel. I simply could not believe this eminent scientist had said that the universe had "exploded into being." What was it before it exploded into being? In historic categories, being is the antithesis of nonbeing, and nonbeing is a synonym for nothing.

What is nothing? In all my years of philosophical inquiry, I never found an adequate definition of nothing—until R. C. Jr. went to junior high school. That was when I finally came to an understanding of its meaning.

It turned out that nothing was what he did in school everyday. He'd come home and I'd say, "What did you do in school today?" and he would say, "Nothing."

Nothing is so obviously the absence of something that philosophers cannot even talk about what it is, only about what it is not. But in the most basic categories, nothing is the absence of being. As I've said until my congregation is tired of hearing it, if there ever were a time when nothing at all existed, what could possibly exist now? Nothing. But if something exists now, that tells you indisputably that there *never* was a time when there was nothing—not twelve billon years ago, not eighteen billion years ago, not eighteen *trillion* years ago.

Everything that we know of, including the universe itself, had a beginning, which means it is contingent, derived, dependent on something outside of itself to lend being to it—except for God. God was not created. There was never a time when He was not. He derived His being not from something before Him or something outside of Him but from Himself. He has the power of being in and of Himself. I wish everybody had a chance to delve into the depths of the inquiries of Western philosophy to explore the concept of being, because there is nothing more profound to say about God than that which He says about Himself when He reveals Himself by the name "I AM WHO I AM" (Ex. 3:14).

This was the message God communicated to Cyrus when He said, "I am the LORD, and there is no other." He was saying: "I alone, Cyrus, have the power of being within myself. Apart from Me, Cyrus, you couldn't exist for a second. You couldn't possibly live apart from My being, because it is in Me that you live and move and have your being. I am the LORD; there is no other."

Ontologically and Logically Necessary

Thomas Aquinas bequeathed to the Western world all kinds of well-known arguments for the existence of God, some of which have been blatantly ignored by modern evangelicals—to their impoverishment. But I think the most compelling argument was, first of all, the *ens necessarium*, the idea that God possesses "necessary being." He alone has being that is necessary. What in the world does that mean? Perhaps I should ask, "What *beyond* the world does that mean?" because there is nothing on this planet or in this universe apart from God that possesses necessary being.

We can define necessary being in two ways, ontologically and logically. Aquinas argued for both. Ontology is the study of being or the science of being, so when Aquinas said that God has necessary being, he was saying that God is the kind of being who cannot possibly *not* be. God is who He is from everlasting to everlasting, and He cannot be anything other than what He is. If He could be something other than what He is, He would have to change, and if He changed, He would stop being God.

One of my favorite hymns is "And Can It Be That I Should Gain" by Charles Wesley. I love that hymn, except for one small part. The refrain asks the question, "How can it be that thou, my God, shouldst die for me?" Charles Wesley, shame on you. Do you really mean to say that God died on the cross? How could God suffer an end to His being? If the being of God had perished on the cross, the cross would have perished with Him. The hill outside of Jerusalem would have been vaporized and Jerusalem would have vanished along with the whole of creation, because apart from the being of God, nothing can exist for a split second. No, God did not die. The God-man died. The God who took on Himself a human nature died in His humanity, but the deity did not perish on the cross. To speak of God dying may sound great in Wesley's hymn, but it's a ghastly thought, because God has necessary being, which cannot stop being. He is ontologically necessary.

But what has been almost completely lost in our day is the truth that His being is not only ontologically necessary, it is logically necessary. There is no reason that I can offer why R. C. Sproul should exist. There was a time when I didn't exist. There was a time when you didn't exist.

Neither you nor I can claim any logical necessity for our existence. But not only is God ontologically necessary, you have to take leave of reason, park your rationality in the parking lot, and deposit your scientific certainty there as soon as you begin to explore the idea that God does not exist. You have to stop thinking logically to argue that the universe came into being by itself, out of nothing. When you talk like that, in the name of science, you've just traded in science for ignorance and nonsense. Nothing could be more irrational than the idea that something comes from nothing.

I once read an article by a Nobel prize-winning physicist, who said that the time had come to give up the ancient idea that we can explain the origin of the universe through spontaneous generation. Through scientific investigation, he said, we now know that things cannot come out of nothing spontaneously. But he went on to say: "For something to come into being out of nothing requires time. You can't get something out of nothing quickly. You have to have patience. You have to wait on it." This is an act of pulling a rabbit out of a hat—without a rabbit, without a hat, and without a magician. That's not science, that's nonsense. That's mythology. Logic demands that if something exists now, something has always existed, or you have to choose an irrational alternative. That is what Aquinas was getting at. God not only has ontologically necessary being, He has logically necessary being.

Well-being and Calamity

While this is a brief portrait of who God is, as He presented Himself to Cyrus, I want us to consider what God does. He says: "I am the LORD, and there is no other, besides me there is no God; I equip you, though you do not know me, that people may know, from the rising of the sun and from the west, that there is none beside me; I am the LORD and there is no other" (vv. 5–6). Then comes verse 7: "I form light and create darkness, I make well-being and create calamity, I am the LORD, who does all these things."

This verse has created problems for people who rely on the King James Version, which translates the verse this way: "I form the light, and create darkness: I make peace, and create evil: I the LORD do all these things." You can see the difficulty here. I've had many students come to me with their KJV Bibles and say: "You teach us that the biblical *a priori* is that God is not the author of evil, and yet, here it is, right in my Bible: 'I am the LORD. . . . I create evil.'"

When that happens, I explain that we can look at this text in terms of the words employed or we can look at it in terms of the poetic structure of the passage, which happens to be a case of parallelism, a common Jewish literary form. In this case, it's antithetical parallelism. God makes light and God makes darkness. God brings prosperity and God brings evil. The terms are antithetical. They are opposites.

The Hebrew word that is translated as "calamity" in the English Standard Version and as "evil" in the King James has a multitude of meanings, stretching all the way from food that tastes nasty to full-orbed moral evil. In this case, the parallelism and the context indicate that God is saying: "Cyrus, I am the Lord. There is no other. I form the light. I bring the darkness. I bring well-being. I create calamity."

Immediately after the devastating terrorist attacks of September 11, 2001, bumper stickers appeared saying, "God bless America." At the same time, it seemed as if everyone in the world asked me as a theologian, "Where was God on 9/11?" I said: "He was in the same place he was on 9/10 and on 9/12. He didn't move." They would then ask, "How can God allow these things to happen?" Pat Robertson and Jerry Falwell unwisely said that the destruction the terrorists wreaked was the judgment of God on the United States. The hue and cry of the people of this country and the news media was so severe that Robertson and Falwell recanted their statements. It was unthinkable to the American people that God could have had anything to do with that calamity. We are a people who believe that God can bless a nation, but we refuse to accept the idea that God can judge a nation.

The reason for that dichotomy, I believe, is that we don't know who God is. The God of popular religion is not holy. He is not the God who is introduced here in Isaiah, the God who brings the bull market and the bear market, who raises up kings and brings them down.

The two books that I have written that have received the most response are *The Holiness of God* and *Chosen by God*. Many people have said to me: "You know, your book *The Holiness of God* just blew me away. It gave me an exalted view of the majesty of God. Then I read *Chosen by God*, but I didn't like that one at all."

When I get those comments, I usually say: "Either you didn't understand *The Holiness of God* or you didn't understand *Chosen by God*. The God who is holy is the God who is sovereign. The God who is transcendent in His majesty is the omnipotent Lord. He brings good things and He brings bad things." Job understood that when he said, "The LORD gave, and the LORD has taken away; blessed be the name of the LORD" (Job 1:21b).

This is the God with whom we have to deal—whether we like Him or not. He is God, He alone. That is what He said to Cyrus: "I am the LORD." You might prefer a different god. You might even try to fashion one. But there is no other.

Note

1 John Calvin, *The Institutes of the Christian Religion*, trans. Henry Beveridge, revised edition (Peabody, Mass.: Hendrickson Publishers, 2008), 3.21.3.

"HALLOWED BE YOUR NAME":
THE HOLINESS OF THE FATHER

- Sinclair B. Ferguson -

THE SEVENTEENTH CHAPTER OF JOHN'S GOSPEL takes us to a holy place where Christ introduces us to the holy Father:

> When Jesus had spoken these words, he lifted up his eyes to heaven, and said, "Father, the hour has come; glorify your Son that the Son may glorify you, since you have given him authority over all flesh, to give eternal life to all whom you have given him. And this is eternal life, that they may know you the only true God, and Jesus Christ whom you have sent. I glorified you on earth, having accomplished the work that you gave me to do. And now, Father, glorify me in your own presence with the glory that I had with you before the world existed. . . . All mine are yours, and yours are mine, and I am

glorified in them. And I am no longer in the world, but they are in the world, and I am coming to you. Holy Father, keep them in your name, which you have given me, that they may be one, even as we are one. . . . Sanctify them in the truth; your word is truth. As you sent me into the world, so I have sent them into the world. And for their sake I consecrate [or sanctify] myself, that they also may be sanctified in truth. I do not ask for these only, but also for those who will believe in me through their word, that they may all be one, just as you, Father, are in me, and I in you, that they also may be in us, so that the world may believe you have sent me. . . . Father, I desire that they also, whom you have given me, may be with me where I am, to see my glory that you have given me because you loved me before the foundation of the world. O righteous Father, even though the world does not know you, I know you, and these know that you have sent me. I made known to them your name, and I will continue to make it known, that the love with which you have loved me may be in them, and I in them." (vv. 1–5, 10–11, 17–21, 24–26)

In many ways, it would be much easier to write about the holiness of God, about which the Scriptures have a great deal to say, than to address the subject of the holy Father. If the truth be told, we are not really accustomed to thinking specifically of the holiness of the Father *as Father*. This itself underlines the fact that often when we speak about the holiness of God we are still thinking in a man-centered fashion in this sense: we speak of Him as being "separate from us." But we are then thinking thoughts centered in ourselves rather than in Him.

When, however, we speak about the holiness of the Father as Father, we must begin with God the Trinity. The holiness of the Father is not an attribute He adopts, as it were, only when He creates. If He is the holy Father, He is ever so, and indeed must have been so before all worlds in the ineffable mystery of the eternal in-being and fellowship of the Trinity. The fathers of the church expounded this relationship in terms of what they called the divine *perichoresis* (from the Greek verb *perichōreō*, "to go around, come around, go to in succession"). The Father, the Son, and the Spirit are always engaged in mutually dynamic relationships and fellowship within the unity of Their threeness. Within that relationship, each person is "holy." It is tempting to think that the seraphim are in such constant awe in the presence of God because they are privileged to sense this mystery—and feel they are not fit to gaze on it without winged protection—so they cry, "Holy, holy, holy is the LORD of hosts" (Isa. 6:3).

It is part of the mystery of the incarnation, as John expresses it in the prologue to his Gospel, that this fellowship remains unbroken throughout our Lord's earthly ministry. The *Logos* (Word) is always "at the Father's side" (literally "in the Father's bosom") and "has made him known" (literally "he has exegeted him," John 1:18). This is underlined in John 17:11 by the single occurrence of the words "holy Father" in the entire New Testament.

It would be challenging enough to ask, "What would we mean if we addressed God in prayer as 'holy Father'?" But to ask, "What did Jesus mean?" is to enter what is, for most of us, uncharted territory and to feel that we have a privilege hitherto reserved for seraphim. John 17 is holy ground, and, at least metaphorically, we need to take off our shoes if we are to walk on it.

Our Lord's prayer here comes not only at the high point theologically in the Gospel, but also the deepest point emotionally and affectionally in His life and ministry. In a sense, He is, as He says here, "no longer in the world" (v. 11). The die is cast. He is going to the cross and to the Father. The apostle John records words here that he does not record Jesus saying anywhere else as he sets before us the poignant scene in which Jesus pours out His soul before His heavenly Father, desiring His glory in His Father's presence, desiring the blessing and salvation of His beloved disciples, and expressing His last will and testament: that the whole church, which He will purchase with His blood, will see Him in His glory (17:24).

With heightened intensity, the Lord prays. Six times He addresses God as Father. But only once do the words "holy Father" form on His lips. This is what the grammarians call a "hapaxlegomenon," a word or statement that is made once in a body of literature and does not appear again.

It is challenging to us mentally and spiritually to grasp what Jesus means when He addresses God in this way. Perhaps the sheer immensity of this title is indicated by the fact that in your personal prayer and in corporate prayer led by the leadership in your church, this may be the least frequently (if ever) used mode of address to God—"O holy Father." It behooves us, therefore, to come up gently on this title, as though we were conscious that we are little boys and girls about to explore something so intimate, so sacred, that we are endangered—as indeed we are endangered—by exploring what it meant for Jesus to say, "holy Father," and then to invite us to pray in like language: "When you pray, say: Our Father in heaven, Hallowed be Your name'" (Luke 11:2, NKJV).

Unfolding Mysteries

We are helped to do this when we understand that the Gospel of John divides neatly into two halves. Scholars debate as to exactly where the division comes. But there comes a point in the twelfth chapter when Jesus withdraws from the world and does no more signs, except the manifestation of His great name, the "I AM." Thus ends what some commentators have described as the "book of the signs" (chaps. 1–12), as Jesus withdraws to disclose the intimate truths of grace to His disciples in what is likewise sometimes called the "book of glory" (chaps. 13–21).

Every reader of the Gospels is conscious of a difference in style between the first three (often called the "Synoptic" Gospels because they share a common approach and viewpoint) and the Gospel of John. John Calvin sums this up cleverly when he writes that since all the Gospels "had the same object, to show Christ, the first three exhibit His body, if I may be permitted to put it like that, but John shows his soul."[1]

This emerges from John 13 onward as Jesus begins to teach His disciples.

16

He unfolds mysteries that they struggle to grasp. Even then, He says, "I still have many things to say to you, but you cannot bear them now" (16:12). But while that is true, He begins to bring them, in fellowship and in ministry, to a deeper knowledge of the ineffable mystery of God the Trinity.

This—at least for me—is the ultimate evidence that for John the Trinity is not the most speculative and most impractical doctrine, as it often seems to be for Christians today. In fact, if this is what Jesus teaches His disciples when He—and they with Him—stand under such great stress, then this must be the *least speculative* doctrine in the Bible, and, at the end of the day, it must be the *most practical*. After all, if they love Him they will not only want to keep His commandments (14:21), they also will want to know Him better. He thus brings them to understand the ministry of the Holy Spirit, through whom this intimate knowledge will be theirs. He not only brings them in to understand the identity of the heavenly Father, but also to appreciate His own relationship with Him. "In that day," He says, with a reference to Pentecost, "you will know that I am in my Father, and you in me, and I in you" (14:20).

If the language had not been abused elsewhere, I think we could write as a heading over John 13–17, "The sacred heart of Christ." If you want to know Jesus Christ, then you must have at least a basic working knowledge of what He teaches His disciples in this Farewell Discourse.

Fascinatingly, this discourse begins with a parable of descent, as Jesus rises from supper, disrobes, and stoops down to wash His disciples' dirty feet. Knowing that He has come from the Father and is going to the Father, He gives His disciples an acted parable of His gracious work of atonement (13:1–20). But the whole section also ends with a parable of ascent, or better, a prayer of ascent, as Jesus comes to the Father, praying that He will be able to glorify His Father's name and that His Father will glorify Him (John 17). Here we are able to eavesdrop on things that are almost illegitimate for man to utter.

Marvelously, then, He prays that the disciples, who are about to see Him in His abject humiliation, will be kept by the holy name of the Father to see Him in His magnificent glory: "Father, I desire that they also, whom you have given me, may be with me where I am, to see my glory that you have given me because you loved me before the foundation of the world" (v. 24). His desire is that those He knows and loves best, and who—despite all their failings—love Him best in return, although they now realize He is "despised and rejected by men; a man of sorrows, and acquainted with grief" (Isa. 53:3), should see Him exalted, crowned, glorified—home. Only then does He go out to fulfill the atoning work of His death and resurrection.

Here is the link to us. When He rises in the early morning of His resurrection day, He charges Mary Magdalene to say, "Go to my brothers and say to them, 'I am ascending to my Father and your Father, to my God and your God'" (20:17). Although His words are sometimes interpreted as though Jesus were building a chasm between His relationship with the Father and our relationship with the Father, the reverse is almost certainly the truth. In and through His resurrection, He is, as it were, beginning to gather children, from all the ends of the earth, into the worldwide, eternity-long family of God. And He is inviting us similarly, as we shall see, to come to God and say far more frequently than we are wont to do, "O holy Father."

An Eternal Address

What does it mean for the Lord of glory to come to the Father and say "holy Father"? The eternal Word, the Son of God, has, from all eternity, in all eternity, and through all eternity, always addressed the Father as "holy Father." What does that mean? What does it mean that from all eternity in the blessed Trinity there has been this response of the eternal Son to His eternal Father—a response to the Father's person in which the Son's instinct has been to address Him, as He does at this high point of emotion, as "holy Father"?

When we speak about the attributes of God, as orthodox Christians

18

do, we must understand that for something to be an essential divine attribute, it must have been exercised before all worlds. In fact, for something properly to be called an attribute of God, it must have been expressed and experienced in the most intense and dynamic forum among the three persons of the Trinity—when the Father with His Son in the union of the Holy Spirit were all that was.

In this sense, technically speaking, the wrath of God is not an essential attribute of God. God indeed expresses wrath. But that wrath of God is a fundamental attribute of God coming to expression in the temporal context of the fall and human sinfulness. It did not come to expression within the blessed Trinity; having no object for its exercise, it had no existence in God's person. In fact, wrath is the expression of an eternal divine attribute when the eternal comes into contact with the sinful.

But the holiness of God *did* come to expression. God is worshiped in sinless glory for His holiness. So when Jesus says "holy Father," what He says here on earth expresses the heart of the Son who has gazed on the face of His blessed Father from all eternity, revealing that His instinct has been to praise Him, to admire Him, and to love Him because of His perfect holiness.

That means that whatever the semantics of the biblical terms for holiness may be, the *meaning* of holiness cannot be "separation." With respect to the creation and especially the human creature, the meaning of holiness becomes separation from the creation and from the sinner. But within the blessed fellowship of the divine Trinity, the meaning of "holy" must be, shall we say, "purity." Scholars have seen the notion of the numinous, the awe-inspiring, bound up with this idea. Perhaps we could even say it involves "intensity." In the Father, holiness is a purity of an infinite intensity and beauty that creates a sense of awe and wonder in the spectator.

Though we are almost driven to think in terms of divine attributes as entities in themselves (thus we see love, righteousness, and holiness as abstractable qualities), the truth is that God is simple in His being. He is all that He is in everything He is. Thus, divine holiness is His infinitely intense purity as the God who is not complex but simple. His holiness is His love, righteousness, and faithfulness—the infinite intensity of all that He is in the unity of His fatherly being with reference to His beloved Son, so that as His Son looks on Him, His Son's response is to say, "O holy Father." To both the Son and the Spirit, the Father is truly awesome. In a human relationship, a man might see his wife appearing after readying herself for a formal social event and find that the sight of her takes his breath away in admiration and love. To be "awestruck" in this sense is not the sign of being an inferior being or person, but rather that sense of wonder at beauty and dignity that is enhanced by the very fact that the husband knows that this woman belongs to him and has a love for him that is unique.

It is in this sense, surely magnified greatly, that there is a sense of profound personal awe when our Lord breathes the words "holy Father."

This is a place we can scarcely go. We turn to Isaiah 6 and see the prophet responding to the expressions of the divine holiness as he feels himself undone. As we read through Isaiah 5 into Isaiah 6, we find a very specific pattern emerging: Isaiah pronounces a series of woes on sinners. There are six of them (5:8, 11, 18, 20, 21, 22). Given the biblical fascination with the number seven, we are led to expect that a final woe is yet to come. But we have no way of anticipating against whom it will be pronounced. So it is to our astonishment that the prophet pronounces it *on himself.* "Woe is me! For I am lost" (Isa. 6:5). Catching a glimpse of the true worship of the Holy One overwhelms him and undoes him. Correspondingly, the reason we are not undone is not because we are purer than God's prophet; it is because we have so little sense of whom we address when we take on our lips the address "holy Father."

The truth is we know we are not fit to say "holy Father." But when we gaze on the seraphim of Isaiah's vision, we find something possibly even more unexpected. These seraphim, who have never sinned, who are holy, as they sense the intensity of God's attributes being expressed toward them out of the heart of the divine being, are constrained to veil their faces and cover their feet. Although perfectly holy, they dare not look directly on the intensity of the holiness of the heavenly Father without danger, if not certainty, of disintegration.

It is in stark yet glorious contrast to this that we find John opening his Gospel by saying, "In the beginning was the Word, and the Word was with God" (*pros ton theon*—literally "toward God").

Do you see the picture here? If the Son is "toward God," He must be face to face with Him—alone (with the Spirit) able to bear the intensity of the Father's gaze. That face is all-consuming love, and burns to destruction all in the object of its gaze that is not itself perfect love. Thus, He gazes on His Son. All creatures must cover their faces or avert their eyes. Only the Son (always in and with the Spirit) is able to love in return with an intensity that preserves Him from being consumed by the holiness of the Father.

My sense of biblical revelation is that God has made us not only to have communion with Him, but in such a way that we can grasp and appreciate what that communion is like. This is in measure the meaning of the biblical doctrine of our creation as the image of God. But further, embedded within this are further echoes of the in-being of God in the mutual being of man and woman.

Perhaps a personal illustration here will make the point. By far my most intimate relationship in all the world is with my wife. No man else may lock eyes with my wife and gaze at her the way I am privileged to do and say, "I love you with all of my being." Doubtless we use the word in a weakened sense, but it is nevertheless employed in a real sense when we speak about "holy" matrimony. It is the sphere in which there can exist an almost devouring intensity of desire to possess and be possessed (but never one without the other). Unless the love is mutual, the holiness of desire on the part of the one will destroy the relationship.

But there is a further dimension to this analogy. Those who thus love are capable of spending extraordinary amounts of time with one another doing "little more" than enjoying one another's company—whether few or many words are exchanged. Love in its most heightened relationships is satisfied by and with the beloved.

The holiness of love that flows between the Father and Son in the Spirit is infinitely greater than the most intense human devotion and holy passion. The blessed Son is able to gaze into the eyes of the holy heavenly Father and bear in His being, in the mystery of His eternal being, the intensity of the Father's holy love for Him and desire for fellowship with Him so that "the deep things" of God with respect to each person are fully unveiled and enjoyed. That is the intensity of the Father's desire to have fellowship with Him.

As is well known, Augustine in his *Confessions* tells of a questioner demanding to know, "What was God doing before he made heaven and earth?" He is content to say that he does not know, although he admits he is familiar with the more famous and facetious answer, "He was preparing Hell for people who pry into mysteries."[2] Apparently Calvin found the answer more apt than his master.[3]

But surely—if a cat may look at two kings—neither of them provided the right answer. The answer is that He was enjoying His Son in and with the Spirit. That which the image—male and female—may experience intensely in the wonder of mutual devotion and satisfaction, the Eternal One knows within the inter-personal relationships of the Trinity.

Seeing the Father in the Son

John records our Lord speaking of the nature of His relationship with the Father as being "in" the Father: "you, Father, are in me, and I in you" (John 17:21). This is the ground of our union with the Father.

These words of our Lord unveil great depths of truth while simultaneously underlining that while we can grasp this we cannot comprehend it all. The Father is in the Son and the Son is in the Father. As the incarnate Son, Jesus, gives expression to the relationship that He has with the Father, He longs, as He says in verse 24, to return from His state of humiliation to His state of exaltation. He longs also that we may be there to see Him as He is, to stand, as it were, on the sidelines and observe, and taste the glory.

Since no man can see God and live, the only way we can do this (for that matter, the only way the seraphim can ever do this) is by indirect means—by seeing the glory of God in the face of Jesus Christ. We cannot look into the eyes of the Father and hold our gaze, as though we had access to His eternal being. Rather, we must, as it were, stand on the circumference and watch the eyes of the God-man Jesus Christ as He gazes on His heavenly Father. In this we are like those who take the greatest delight and pleasure in seeing two lovers "made for each other" engaging in a human *perichoresis* of mutual affection, admiration, and devotion that is marked by open self-giving to one another and total satisfaction in one another. When we see the face of the Father reflected in the eager eyes of His Son incarnate, then we find ourselves worshiping and ever crying with the seraphim, and with all the choristers of heaven, "Holy, holy, holy is the LORD of hosts," as though we were witnessing the display of a trillion laser beams of light, pure and intense.

Sometimes we mistakenly think that what most causes awe and reverence before God is the threat of His holiness, the fear of His law, and the terror of judgment and condemnation. But it is not so. Pure and intense love has more power to effect awe, even gracious fear, than all terror.

Have you ever felt that someone cared so much that you should be the best you can be that you needed to turn away? Often, as a student, spending time with someone who cared deeply that I should belong without reservation to Christ, honor Him throughout my life, and use whatever gifts I might have for the glory of God, I found myself experiencing a strange paradox—leaving the person's presence with a longing to be in it again and yet inwardly running lest all this prove so costly that my life would no longer be under my own sway.

That is what we get a touch of here. We cannot gaze directly on the Father—but, says Jesus, "Whoever has seen me has seen the Father. . . .

Do you not believe that I am in the Father and the Father is in me?" (John 14:9–10). As the Lord Jesus comes to His heavenly Father, He gives us a little sense of the extraordinary intimacy between the Father and Son as He looks on Him and says, "holy Father."

Perhaps the simplest analogy is this. You are a young student who has just fallen in love. You return to your dorm. Your friends, who know the name of the girl you were with, want to know where you have been and what you have been doing for the past four hours. You say, "We haven't actually been doing anything." Then they say, "You can't spend four hours not doing anything." But to yourself you say: "I have never experienced anything quite like this! I feel I could explore her mind and soul without intermission. And even then I feel there would be more to know and adore."

Think of it. We are finite, distorted human beings, but in the exploration of one another, we find such glorious temporal satisfaction. If that can be true of the image God created male and female, how much more true of God Himself? He thus provides us with a simple, yet astonishingly common, analogy of that which is beyond our comprehension.

Incidentally, Scripture underlines for us that *being* is fundamental to *doing*. But we've reversed that in our day. For us, doing has become the more important thing. People sometimes ask me, "What do you and your wife like to do?" I always say: "We don't like to do anything. We just like to be together." They'll say, "But what do you do when you're together?" "Well," I say, "we sometimes talk and we sometimes sit in silence." Again they'll inquire, "But what do you *like* to do?" The truth of the matter is that I just like to look at my wife and ponder how it can be that she has devoted her life to me.

In considering what Jesus meant when He said "holy Father," we do well to follow Calvin, who said, "When [God] sets an end to teaching . . . stop trying to be wise."[4] Rather than stand in perplexity and say, "I need to understand this," let it suffice us that we can overhear the words of our Lord Jesus Christ and be lost in wonder, love, and praise that we have had a glimpse of this ineffable relationship between the Father and His Son.

A Glorious New Relationship

It is against this background that John's Gospel then brings us into what the relationship between the Father and the Son must have been in all eternity and continues to be today.

Throughout His ministry, the Son remained in the bosom (perhaps even "in the lap") of His Father. The amazing thing is that He became flesh. The Word, who was face to face with God, in the bosom of the Father, became flesh. Why did He become flesh? Let the answer bring a sense of awe to our hearts: He became flesh to bring us into the same relationship to the holy Father that He experienced and enjoyed in the finitude and weakness of the flesh in which He was incarnated.

Of the many wonderful insights John's Gospel gives us into this relationship, two seem to me especially marvelous.

The first is in John 5:19–20. Here, Jesus is speaking about His relationship with His Father and says, "Truly, truly, I say to you, the Son can do nothing of his own accord, but only what he sees the Father doing." This shows us the way He lived as a Son. We can imagine that Jesus lived this way with Joseph, watching His earthly father making the yoke for the ox or tables for the neighborhood homes, and learning to be a carpenter.

The second, expressed from the other side of the relationship (that is, from the perspective of the Father's attitude to the Son), is in John 10:17, when Jesus speaks about giving His life for the sheep. "For this reason," He says, "the Father loves me, because I lay down my life that I may take it up again."

Luke tells us that Jesus, the Incarnate One, actually grew in favor with the holy Father (Luke 2:40). Indeed, unless our Jesus is a Jesus who grew physically, grew in wisdom, *but also grew in favor with His heavenly Father*, our Jesus is not the Jesus of the New Testament. As the pressures mounted and became the more challenging and demanding, and as He had opportunity to demonstrate greater and greater obedience until He was obedient unto death, even the death of the cross, Jesus gave hints of the inner mystery of His relationship to His Father. Even when He was under the judgment of His heavenly Father—no, *especially* when He was under the judgment of God—His heavenly Father was surely singing, "My Jesus, I love thee, I know thou art mine; . . . *if ever I loved thee, my Jesus, 'tis now*."[5]

Is it not almost unbearable to think of such devotion on the part of the Son to His beloved Father—and of the Father's heart-breaking admiration and love for His Son?

All of this, you see, is to bring us lost, broken sinners into fellowship with God so that we can say, as John says, in essence, in his first letter, "Here is the mystery of the blessing of the gospel, that our fellowship is in the power of the Spirit, through the Son, with the holy Father" (see 1 John 1:1–3). As our Lord Jesus leads us and gives us access to the presence of God, we want to hide behind Jesus. But He says, "Now, My child, come from behind Me, and watch My eyes as I gaze into the eternal heart of My Father and say, 'Holy Father, here am I, and the children You have given Me'" (see Heb. 2:13).

The Privileges of the Relationship

That is our privilege, because, of course, the Scriptures teach us that we have been brought into this family. So what might it mean for me, for you, and for us as the people of God to be able to come to Him in the name of the Lord Jesus and say to Him, "holy Father"?

Notice three very simple things:

First, if we say "Our holy Father" when we pray, that means that the church, which He purchased with His own blood, is the holy family. Years ago, in the church I served in Glasgow, Scotland, I was preaching one Sunday night on the Trinity, and halfway through the sermon, a whole crowd of people from the Near East trooped into the gallery of the church. I remember thinking: "Help—Muslims are here because they know I am preaching on the Trinity. Perhaps I will be here for a long time

26

afterwards engaged in debate and defense!" If I remember rightly, all of the late arrivals were from Egypt. They were educators sent over by the Egyptian government. Half of those in the group were, in fact, Muslims, but those who had come to the service were Coptic Christians. Some of them I found to be strikingly Christ-centered. Others, however, were what I would call "traditionalists."

Afterward, one of them asked me, "Did you know the holy family came to Egypt?"

"Yes," I replied, "I know they went to Egypt. We read of this in Matthew's Gospel. Indeed we know they went to Egypt." But I also wanted to say: "Dear friend—*this congregation here is the holy family.*"

We see this in the early chapters of the Acts of the Apostles. One of the great paradoxes in Acts is that the holiness of the Father so dawns on the early believers as to fill the community with such awe that we are told nobody dared join that church (Acts 5:13). Do you belong to a church like that—a church that some people avoid not because people within the church crack the whip, but because God is in the midst of His people as the holy Father? Yet—astonishingly—the very next verse says, "And more than ever believers were added to the Lord" (Acts 5:14). That is what it means when a congregation of the Lord becomes the holy family. There is something about that community that expresses the holiness of the Father, and that makes outsiders feel "there is no way I could be worthy to be part of that." Yet, at the same time, they long with all their hearts to find that family that is the true and great family of the heavenly Father.

Second, this understanding should permeate our worship. Some of us are good at family and some of us feel we are better at what we think to be "holiness." But not many of our churches are good at being holy families. Yet when we begin to reflect the fatherhood of God among us, that is what we become. So when we come to God, we say, "Our Father in heaven, hallowed be your name" (Matt. 6:9). Since He is the holy Father, as Paul says, He gives His children the Holy Spirit, who "bears witness with our spirit that we are children of God" (Rom. 8:17). With this assurance, we cry out, "Abba, Father" (v. 15). That is not a cry reserved for the greatest and the most sanctified, but given to the most deeply hurt. He wants us to know in our deepest distress as we cry out to Him that He is our Father and that He cares for us.

Third, since He is the holy Father, He has set His heart on making all of His children like His holy Son. Since He has given His Son to death that that might take place, He will not stop "till all the ransomed church of God be saved to sin no more."[6]

The privilege of this dawns on us only when we remember how much it cost Jesus to enable us to say "holy Father" and to provide for us the clearest evidence of the sheer intensity of the Father's holiness, which was found when He appeared before His Father bearing our sins in His own body on the tree and said, "Holy Father, smite the Shepherd." In the intensity of His admiration for His holy Son—"If ever I loved thee, my Jesus, 'tis now"—He smote the Shepherd, in order that the sheep might be gathered through Him who was "wounded for our transgressions; . . . crushed for our iniquities; upon him was the chastisement that brought us peace, and with his stripes we are healed" (Isa. 53:5).

Oh, what a privilege it is to say "holy Father."

Notes

1 John Calvin, *The Gospel According to St. John*, trans. T. H. L. Parker, eds. D. W. and T. F. Torrance (Edinburgh: Saint Andrew Press, 1959), 6.

2 Augustine, *Confessions* (Harmondsworth, Middlesex, England: Penguin Books, 1961), Book 11, chapter 12.

3 John Calvin, *Institutes of the Christian Religion*, Library of Christian Classics, vols. XX–XXI, ed. John T. McNeill, trans. Ford Lewis Battles (Louisville: Westminster John Knox, 1960), 1.14.1.

4 Ibid., 3.21.3.

5 From the hymn "My Jesus, I Love Thee" by William R. Featherstone, 1864 (emphasis added).

6 From the hymn "There Is a Fountain Filled with Blood" by William Cowper, 1772.

3

"THE HOLY ONE OF GOD":

THE HOLINESS
OF JESUS

- Steven J. Lawson -

As we consider the holiness of our Lord Jesus Christ, I can think of no better place to turn in the Scriptures than to Mark 1. Consider this text and set it before your mind and heart, for it speaks pointedly to the holiness of Jesus:

> And they went into Capernaum, and immediately on the Sabbath he entered the synagogue and was teaching. And they were astonished at his teaching, for he taught them as one who had authority, and not as the scribes. And immediately there was in their synagogue a man with an unclean spirit. And he cried out, saying, "What have you to do with us, Jesus of Nazareth? Have you come to destroy us? I know who you are—the Holy One of God." (1:21–24)

There is no more dangerous place to be than where the direct, straight-forward teaching of the Word of God confronts dead religion. As long as dead religion is allowed to sleep the sleep of death, all continues placidly and peaceably. But when the truth of Scripture challenges empty religion, a cataclysmic collision is sure to result. This is because whenever the Word is taught in houses of worship that are devoid of gospel truth, hell is aggravated. As soon as the light of holiness and truth shines into the king-dom of darkness, sin is exposed, unclean spirits are angered, and Satan is provoked. Satan has no greater strongholds than houses of worship where the truth is suppressed. Nowhere is he more deeply entrenched in the lives of people than among those who are religious but who have no supernatural light of holiness and truth. But there is no greater threat to Satan's kingdom than the penetrating light of holiness and truth as it invades these fortresses of demons.

It was in such a dangerous place that Jesus found Himself one day in Capernaum. The synagogue there was a place where Satan had gained a foothold. It was a place that had religion but no repentance; ritual but no regeneration; rules but no relationship with the living God through His holy Son, the Lord Jesus Christ. Make no mistake, it was a ruthlessly religious crowd that most opposed Christ. They attributed His works to the Devil, accused Him of being born out of wedlock, maligned Him, slandered Him, and ultimately nailed Him to a cross. When Jesus fear-lessly advanced with the truth into this bastion of demonic religion, He met the Devil head on. What followed was a clash between light and darkness, truth and error, heaven and hell, and holiness and un-holiness.

A Significant City

Mark tells us first that "they went into Capernaum." The word *they* refers to Jesus and four of the disciples, Simon, Andrew, James, and John. Caper-naum was an exceptionally important city for the Lord. It would become the headquarters of His Galilean ministry. Matthew 9:1 says it eventually became "his own city." Capernaum was in Galilee, on the northwestern shore of the Sea of Galilee. It was a place of much enterprise and was significant in the fishing business. It was situated on the main road that connected Egypt with Mesopotamia, so it was strategically located and highly populous. It also was a military station for Roman soldiers. But when Jesus entered this bustling city, He did not go to any of the businesses or take in the sights. Instead, Mark tells us, "immediately on the Sabbath he entered the synagogue and was teaching" (v. 21b). The word *immediately* is Mark's favorite word to describe the ministry of Jesus—this word appears more than forty times in the Gospel of Mark. This tells us there was a rapid pace and pressing tempo about our Lord's ministry.

The synagogue was a house of worship where people assembled, prayers were offered, and the Scriptures were read and taught. The reading and teaching of the Scriptures was open to any qualified individual selected by the ruler of the synagogue. It was common practice for visiting rabbis—itinerant teachers—to be asked to address the worshipers who gathered in the synagogue. That is what happened here—Jesus was invited to teach, and that is exactly what He began to do. He had come to save sinners on the cross, but He also had come to be the chief revelation of God to man. Having been anointed in the power of the Holy Spirit at the Jordan River, He came to this house of worship to open the Word of God for the people. When He did, gospel light shone brightly, piercing the depths of darkness in this synagogue.

Fifteen times in Mark's Gospel we read that Jesus devoted Himself to the ministry of teaching. Twelve times in Mark's Gospel Jesus is identified as "the Teacher." His primary approach in ministry was to read, teach, and apply the Word. It was a straightforward ministry; there were no superficial frills, no mindless beating around the bush. He would open the Scriptures, and divine exposition of the holy truth would come pouring forth from His lips. He *was* the great Expositor.

What was the reaction of those in the synagogue? "They were astonished at his teaching" (v. 22a). The people had been in realms of darkness while the light of truth had been hidden under a bushel. But now, for this moment in time, the bushel was removed, and Christ, the Light of the World, expounded the unadulterated truth of the Word of God like they had never heard it before. Mark says they were "astonished" or "amazed," which is an incredibly strong word. It literally means they were "struck out of themselves" or "out of their senses." We would say, in the vernacular, that what they heard "blew their minds." Jesus' teaching was utter "shock and awe." They were astonished, overwhelmed with the powerful flow of truth that came to them.

The astonishing thing about Jesus' teaching was this: "he taught them as one who had authority, and not as the scribes" (v. 22b). The scribes and the Pharisees would scratch their chins and say, "Well, it seems to me . . ." They would quote other rabbis and scribes. They majored on minors, the minutia of their man-made religious rules and petty legalistic requirements, which placed such heavy burdens on the shoulders of the people. But Jesus stood up and said, "Thus says the Lord." He accurately proclaimed the Word of God in the purest exposition that has ever been heard. But it was not only *what* He said but *how* He said it. Those who heard Him were greatly astonished at the authority with which He taught. They had never heard anything like this unvarnished presentation of truth.

An Unclean Interruption

As the light of truth and holiness shone brilliantly into this dark den of dead religion, "immediately there was in their synagogue a man with an unclean spirit" (v. 23a). Simply put, a demon-possessed man had been sitting in this house of worship. Note that he was not in a house of ill repute. He was not in the harlot's back bedroom. He was not at a drunkard's party. He was in the house of worship, the synagogue, on the Sabbath. To be sure, this was no coincidence, for demons traffic most in religious settings, not least where there is dead religion and a dearth of gospel truth. Jesus spoke of "synagogues of Satan" (Rev. 2:9; 3:9). These are places that may say "house of God" over the portals, but in reality they are held in chains of darkness by a personal Devil, and the people therein are blinded under the dominion and control of demons.

This unclean spirit was a demon residing within the man. Demons are evil spirits that have been cast out of heaven. A third of the angels fell with Lucifer, son of the morning, when he was cast down to this world (Isa. 14:12–13; Rev. 12:4). That is why Satan, now the ruler of this world and the god of this age, has layers of principalities, powers, and rulers of darkness (Eph. 6:12) in his minions here. Demons can live within a human body, causing that person to live a godless, unclean life. In such cases, the demon takes control of the person and speaks through his or her vocal cords, so that when the person is addressed, it is the demon that responds. Unholy demons are agents of Satan—they control minds and corrupt hearts. They are real, and their favorite habitat is houses of worship where there is spiritually dead religion.

This confrontation of light and darkness, holiness and ungodliness, was the perfect storm. Mark tells us, "he cried out" (v. 23b). The "he" refers to the demon. This demon made use of this wretched man's vocal cords and screamed, "What do you have to do with us, Jesus of Nazareth?" (v. 24a). His words literally meant, "What is there between you and us?" In other words, "What do we have in common?" This was a rhetorical question implying a negative answer. There was no common turf. "What fellowship has light with darkness? What accord has Christ with Belial?" (2 Cor. 6:14b–15a). As the demon fearfully stood in the presence of Him who is infinite light, purity, and truth, he realized that he belonged to a totally different world. He was exposed.

Please note the word *us* in verse 24: "What do you have to do with us, Jesus of Nazareth?" This demon was speaking for many demons. Either other demons were in this man, in this synagogue, or scattered about the region. This was a demon-infested place.

This demon then cried out, "Have you come to destroy us?" The demon knew that all fallen angels are under the righteous judgment of

God. Jesus boldly spoke of "the eternal fire prepared for the devil and his angels" (Matt. 25:41). Apparently this demon feared the time had come for his eternal destruction.

Why did he say this? Because there is no question as to the identity of the Lord Jesus Christ in the realms of demon spirits. He said, "I know who you are—the Holy One of God" (v. 24b). That is a better testimony than you will receive from apostate pulpits. Notice that the demon did not speak of "a" Holy One. He used the definite article: "the" Holy One. This foul demon understood that bursting through this veil of human flesh was the absolute, perfect holiness of God in the person of the Lord Jesus Christ. He saw that Jesus of Nazareth was more than a carpenter, more than a mere teacher, more than a mere discipler of men, more than a mere preacher of the Word. He was "Holy, holy, holy . . . the LORD of hosts" (Isa. 6:3). Jesus was holy God in human flesh, fully God and fully man. He was not half God and half man; under such a formula, He would have been a freak. He is one hundred percent God and one hundred percent man, the fully divine Son of the living God. How strange that this high confession should come from such unholy lips, and yet, "The demons believe—and shudder!" (James 2:19).

The Meaning of Holiness

The title "Holy One of God" means that Jesus is infinitely and absolutely holy, fully and perfectly divine. He is transcendent and majestic. He came down from above to save sinners, yet He is set apart from sinners in that He is completely sinless, without any moral blemish, perfect in all of His ways. His being is holy. His character is holy. His mind is holy. His motives are holy. His words are holy. His actions are holy. His ways are holy. His judgments are holy. From the top of His head to the bottom of His feet, every inch, every ounce, the totality, the sum and the substance of the second person of the Godhead is equally holy with God the Father.

What is the holiness of God? First, it has to do with "apart-ness" or "other-ness." The idea of holiness speaks to the profound difference between Him and us. Holiness encompasses His transcendent majesty, His august superiority. He is distinctly set apart from us. As one infinitely above us, He alone is worthy of our worship and our adoration. Moses asked: "Who is like you, O Lord, among the gods? Who is like you, majestic in holiness, awesome in glorious deeds, doing wonders?" (Ex. 15:11). This is the holiness that the demon recognized; he knew that Jesus is the high, lifted-up, supreme being of heaven and earth.

Second, it speaks to His untainted purity, His sinless perfection. God is morally flawless, blameless in all of His ways. The prophet Isaiah stressed this aspect of His character through repeated use of a formal title for God, "the Holy One of Israel." It has been well said that the book of Isaiah is divided into two halves, the first thirty-nine chapters and the last twenty-seven chapters. In the first thirty-nine chapters, this title is found twelve times in reference to God. In the last twenty-seven chapters, this title is found seventeen times. Twenty-nine times in the book of Isaiah, God is identified as "the Holy One of Israel." Some examples include: "They have despised the Holy One of Israel" (1:4); "For great in your midst is the Holy One of Israel" (12:6); and "Your redeemer is the Holy One of Israel" (41:14).

No doubt Isaiah's use of this title flowed out of his encounter with the living God, recorded in Isaiah 6, when he went into the temple and saw the Lord, high and lifted up, and the seraphim surrounding the throne, crying out to one another day and night, "Holy, holy, holy," declaring by their repetition that God is the holiest being, supreme in His holiness in the entire created order. Given that experience, it is no surprise that Isaiah so frequently identified God as the "the Holy One of Israel." Franz Delitzsch, the great Old Testament commentator, writes that this title "forms an essential part of Isaiah's prophetic signature."[1] In other words, this is the unique imprint of Isaiah, stamped on the pages of his book, identifying God as holy again and again.

The Meaning of the Title

When the demon in Mark 1 used a title that was very similar to Isaiah's—"the Holy One of God"—he left no question as to the identification he was making. Let us think about the meaning of this title as applied to the Lord Jesus.

First, it is a title of deity. We have already seen how similar this title is to the title Isaiah assigned to God. In a similar way, God calls Himself "I AM WHO I AM" in Exodus 3:14, then Jesus takes that title to Himself and says, "*I am* the bread of life" (John 6:48), "*I am* the light of the world" (John 8:12), and "*I am* the resurrection and the life" (John 11:25, emphasis added in all references). He takes the divine title of the Old Testament for Himself to show that He is equal to God. Something similar is happening here, though in this case the title for Jesus is voiced by a demon.

The title "Holy One of God" is found in only one other place in the New Testament. When some of Jesus' disciples decided to stop following Him, Jesus asked the Twelve, "Do you want to go away as well?" (John 6:66–67). Peter replied: "Lord, to whom shall we go? You have the words of eternal life, and we have believed, and have come to know, that you are the Holy One of God" (vv. 68–69). With these words, Peter accurately identified their Master as God incarnate, for that is what this title signifies.

Second, it is a title of humble humanity. It acknowledges that the holy God, who is enthroned in the heavens, has come down to be among unholy men. It speaks of the fact that the transcendent, majestic, regal God of heaven has taken on human flesh, yet without sin. Jesus Himself said, "I have come down from heaven" (John 6:38). Jesus was holy God in human form.

Third, it is a title of sinless perfection. If He is God, even though He is a man, Jesus is infinitely pure. Scripture affirms this repeatedly: "In him there is no sin" (1 John 3:5); "He committed no sin, neither was deceit found in his mouth" (1 Peter 2:22); "him . . . who knew no sin" (2 Cor.

5:21). Likewise, Jesus said: "The ruler of this world is coming. He has no claim on me" (John 14:30). The Lord was saying here: "There is no point of access that Satan has gained into My being. He has established no beachhead. There are no satanic strongholds in which he has hatched the poison of hell within Me." He steadfastly resisted every temptation. Jesus could say to His enemies, "Which one of you convicts me of sin?" (John 8:46) because He had no sin.

Triumph over Darkness

Returning to Mark 1, notice how this story plays out. Mark tells us, "Jesus rebuked him, saying, 'Be silent, and come out of him!'" (v. 25). Jesus confronted the demon and called him out. He said: "Shut up, demon! Do not interrupt Me when I am preaching and teaching the Word of the living God." Then, after Jesus commanded the demon to come out, "The unclean spirit, convulsing him and crying out with a loud voice, came out of him" (v. 26). The demon abruptly threw the man into convulsions. The man went into something like an epileptic seizure, probably rolling on the ground and shaking uncontrollably as the unclean spirit burst into this final display of hellish rage. This was a vicious, violent spirit that did not leave quietly.

When the demon finally did come out, "They were all amazed" (v. 27a). The people there in the synagogue already had been amazed by Jesus' teaching; now they experienced amazement upon amazement. They had no category for this. "They questioned among themselves, saying, 'What is this? A new teaching with authority! He commands even the unclean spirits, and they obey him'" (v. 27b). Not only had Jesus preached the sheer unadulterated truth of heaven to them, He had backed it up with all of the authority of God Himself. As a result of their utter astonishment, "At once his fame spread everywhere throughout all the surrounding region of Galilee" (v. 28).

In this confrontation, we see a preview of Jesus' triumph over the kingdom of darkness. The Holy One of God, God in human flesh, "appeared . . . to destroy the works of the devil" (1 John 3:8). As He courageously approached His passion, Jesus said, "Now is the judgment of this world; now will the ruler of this world be cast out" (John 12:31). The Holy One of God went to the cross, where He crushed the head of the Serpent. As a result, "The ruler of this world is judged" (John 16:11).

At Calvary, all of our sins were laid on the sinless Lamb of God, and He gave to us His pure, sinless, perfect obedience to the law of God. This is the great exchange of Calvary: "For our sake he made him to be sin who knew no sin, so that in him we might become the righteousness of God" (2 Cor. 5:21). Jesus had to come as He did, born of a virgin, in order to be what He was, sinless and perfect, in order to do what He, the Holy One, did—die on the cross as the sinless Lamb of God, in order to become sin for us.

Through death, the Bible says, Jesus destroyed the one who has the power of death, the Devil (Heb. 2:14). He bound the strong man, plundered his house at the cross, and set the captives free (Matt. 12:29; Eph. 4:8). His victory shows that "He who is in you is greater than he who is in the world" (1 John 4:4). Therefore, we ought to cry out, "Thanks be to God, who gives us the victory through our Lord Jesus Christ" (1 Cor. 15:57). This victory has come because the Holy One of God came in human flesh to go to the cross and die a death that you and I could never die. Jesus died for us, bearing our sins, suffering under the righteous judgment of God. By His vicarious death and the shedding of His blood, there is full, free forgiveness for our sin. The Holy One of God has come into this unholy world and has scattered the foul kingdom of darkness.

Note

1 C. F. Keil and Franz Delitzsch, *Commentary on the Old Testament in Ten Volumes*, trans. James Martin (repr., Grand Rapids: Eerdmans, 1982), 7:244.

4

"THE BREATH OF THE ALMIGHTY":

THE HOLINESS OF THE SPIRIT

- Alistair Begg -

DESPITE ALL EVIDENCE TO THE CONTRARY, it has been suggested that in 1492, when Columbus sailed the ocean blue, it wasn't just as the history books have it. Some scholars would like us to believe that when Columbus set out, he did not know where he was going; that when he arrived, he did not know where he was; and that when he returned, he did not know where he had been.

An exploration of the nature of the Holy Spirit has the potential to be that kind of a voyage. We can set out without any knowledge of where we are heading, not know where we are when we get there, and not know where we have been when we return.

Jesus said: "The wind blows wherever it pleases. You hear its sound, but you cannot tell where it comes from or where it is going" (John 3:8).

He was speaking of the ministry of the Spirit, but His words could easily describe many examinations of the doctrine of the Spirit. I can attest that in my lifetime, there has been as much confusion within the framework of evangelicalism over the person and work of the Spirit as over any other biblical teaching. Any consideration of any doctrine—but perhaps particularly of the doctrine of the Holy Spirit—that is not grounded within the controls of the Bible may readily and quickly lead to all kinds of flights of fancy.

In his *Institutes of the Christian Religion*, John Calvin writes:

Those who, rejecting Scripture, imagine that they have some peculiar way of penetrating to God, are to be deemed, not so much under the influence of error as madness. For certain giddy men have lately appeared, who, while they make a great display of the superiority of the Spirit, reject all reading of the Scriptures themselves, and deride the simplicity of those who only delight in what they call the dead and deadly letter. But I wish they would tell me what spirit it is whose inspiration raises them to such a sublime height that they dare despise the doctrine of Scripture as mean and childish.[1]

Therefore, I want to set this chapter very clearly within the pages of our Bible, specifically John 16:4b–15:

"I did not say these things to you from the beginning, because I was with you. But now I am going to him who sent me, and none of you asks me, 'Where are you going?' But because I have said these things to you, sorrow has filled your heart. Nevertheless, I tell you the truth: it is to your advantage that I go away, for if I do not go away, the Helper will not come to you. But if I go, I will send him to you. And when he comes, he will convict the world concerning sin and righteousness and judgment: concerning sin, because they do not believe in me; concerning righteousness, because I go to the

Father, and you will see me no longer; concerning judgment because the ruler of this world is judged. I still have many things to say to you, but you cannot bear them now. When the spirit of truth comes, he will guide you into all the truth, for he will not speak on his own authority, but whatever he hears he will speak, and he will declare to you the things that are to come. He will glorify me, for he will take what is mine and he will declare it to you. All that the Father has is mine; therefore I said that he will take what is mine and declare it to you."

Although I might have cited a number of biblical passages, I chose quite arbitrarily to look at this particular section, and particularly at these words of Jesus, which He spoke to the Twelve in the upper room on the night before His crucifixion. The main focus in His words—the necessity of His departure—was in keeping with all that He had been telling them over a period of time, but here He expressed it in a very purposeful and forceful way. This was a matter of consternation and of grief for them, and understandably so.

Jesus had broached the subject earlier in the evening, saying, "Little children, yet a little while I am with you" (13:33). It is significant what Jesus went on to say: "A new commandment I give to you, that you love one another: just as I have loved you, you also are to love one another" (v. 34). Parents, when leaving their children, might say: "We're going away for two weeks, and so and so is going to be looking after you, so make sure you don't fight with one another while we are gone. I don't want to come back and hear that you bickered. I want to hear that you were loving to one another." In a sense, Jesus was the parent and the disciples were the children.

Later, He added, "If you love me, you will keep my commandments" (14:15). Their love for one another was to be grounded in love for Him and revealed in obedient lives. He then went on to say: "If the world hates you, know that it has hated me before it hated you" (15:18). In specific terms, He let them understand that a time was going to come when they actually would be derided and put out of the synagogues.

Given all of this teaching, it's not difficult to see that if ever there was a time when the disciples needed Jesus, if ever there was a time when they wanted His presence, it was surely that night in the upper room. In that context, Jesus explained just why He must leave them.

In this chapter, I want to consider, first, the necessity of Christ's departure; second, the identity of the Helper Jesus promised to send; and third, the activity of this Helper or Counselor.

The Necessity of Christ's Departure

Jesus told His disciples quite clearly what was about to happen: "I did not say these things to you from the beginning, because I was with you. But now I am going to him who sent me" (vv. 4b–5a). But He went on to say, "Nevertheless, I tell you the truth; it is to your advantage that I go away" (v. 7a). Why was that the case? "If I do not go away, the Helper will not come to you. But if I go, I will send him to you" (v. 7b). The disciples were clearly in need of His help, so Jesus let them know that they should not be unduly troubled. Earlier, He had exhorted them: "Let not your hearts be troubled. Believe in God; believe also in me. In my Father's house are many rooms. If it were not so, would I have told you that I go to prepare a place for you? And if I go and prepare a place for you, I will come again and will take you to myself, that where I am you may be also" (14:1–3). Now, in chapter 16, He said: "I don't want you to be unduly troubled because help is on the way. I'm not going to leave you on your own."

It is helpful for us to ponder at what expense this promise was accomplished. Jesus was not simply referring to the pragmatic benefit of the arrival of another Helper. His departure involved all that would happen to Him between the time of this conversation in the upper room and His ascension, after which He would pour out the Holy Spirit as a gift on those to whom He was speaking.

As we reflect on the life and ministry of Jesus, we know that He lived His entire life in union with, and in communion with, the Father. When He was a boy of twelve, Mary and Joseph came looking for Him when He became separated from them on the journey back to Nazareth after the celebration of the Passover in Jerusalem. They found Him in the temple precincts, engaged in conversation with the authoritative scribes and rulers of the day. What must it have been like for Mary and Joseph to find Him there of all places? Mary said, "Behold, your father and I have been searching for you in great distress" (Luke 2:48). Jesus turned and said, "Did you not know that I must be in my Father's house?" (v. 49), or, as the King James Version puts it, "Wist ye not that I must be about my Father's business?" What a strange and enigmatic thing for this twelve-year-old boy to say.

When we read the Gospels carefully, we see that Jesus' sense of intimacy with His Father, an intimacy They shared in eternity before Jesus' incarnation, was pressingly meaningful and precious to Him. Indeed, in the upper room discourse, we find Him again and again referencing His relationship with the Father.

When Jesus prayed in the upper room, His prayer was so impregnated with a sense of intensity, it opened the door, as it were, into the cloistered relationship of the Son and the Father. He said: "Father, the hour has come. . . . Father, glorify me in your own presence. . . . Holy Father, keep them in your name, which you have given me, that they may be one, even as we are one. . . . Father, I desire that they also, whom you have given me, may be with me where I am, to see my glory that you have given me because you loved me before the foundation of the world" (John 17:1, 5, 11, 24). His prayer was filled with references to the Father.

Then, on the cross, He cried, "My God, my God, why have you forsaken me?" (Matt. 27:46). His union and communion with the Father were broken by desertion. He was forsaken of the Father in order that His disciples would not be forsaken. In that peculiar moment on Calvary, He was, if you like, orphaned, in order that those whom He loved and cared for, and those who would be His followers after them, need not live in sorrow.

It was the necessity of His departure that gave rise to this disruption of His relationship with the Father:

How deep the Father's love for us,
How vast beyond all measure
That He should give His only Son
To make a wretch His treasure.

How great the pain of searing loss,
The Father turns His face away
As wounds that mar the chosen One
Bring many sons to glory.[2]

The nature of this necessity lay not simply in the benefit to Jesus' disciples of another Helper, but in the entire drama of redemption, that plan of God formed in the counsels of eternity, a plan that we sometimes refer to as "the covenant of redemption." That which the Father planned, the Son in His death would procure. That which the Son procured, the Spirit—who would come as a Helper, an Advocate, a Counselor, a Comforter, and a Friend—would apply to those for whom Christ died. By the time the apostles wrote their letters, that which was introduced and revealed in the Gospels was being explained. Thus, we read in Colossians and Ephesians that Jesus ascended on high, leading captives in His train and giving gifts to men (Eph. 4:8; Col. 2:15).

That is why, gathered with His disciples in the upper room, He said to them: "I am going to Him who sent Me. I know that you are not quite sure about this. I know that it fills your hearts with sadness. Nevertheless, it is to your advantage that I go away. It is absolutely necessary that I go away, because I have come to do the Father's will, and this is the road I now walk."

The Identity of the Coming Helper

Jesus said: "I tell you the truth: it is to your advantage that I go away, for if I do not go away, the Helper will not come to you. But if I go, I will send him to you" (John 16:7). Now, I don't want to bring cold coals to Newcastle by giving you information with which you are already familiar, so let me just briefly give some background on this verse. You know that the Greek word translated here as "Helper" is *parakletos*. In its technical form, it has a legal dimension; it refers to one who would be an advocate. In its wider context, it speaks of comfort, of protection, of counsel, and of guidance. Jesus also spoke of the Spirit as the Helper in John 14 and introduced Him as "the Spirit of truth" (14:17; 16:13).

I think it best for me to simply say a number of things concerning the identity of this Helper with little embellishment. First, we need to notice that the Holy Spirit is a unique person and not simply a power or an influence. He is spoken of as "He," not as "it." This is a matter of import because if you listen carefully to people speaking, even within your own congregations you may hear the Holy Spirit referenced in terms of the neuter. You may even catch yourself doing it. If you do, I hope you will bite your tongue immediately. We have to understand that the Spirit of God, the third person of the Trinity, is personal. As a person, He may be grieved (Eph. 4:30), He may be quenched in terms of the exercise of His will (1 Thess. 5:19), and He may be resisted (Acts 7:51).

Second, the Holy Spirit is one both with the Father and with the Son. In theological terms, we say that He is both co-equal and co-eternal. When we read the whole Upper Room Discourse, we discover that it was both the Father and the Son who would send the Spirit (John 14:16; 16:7), and the Spirit came and acted, as it were, for both of Them. So the activity of the Spirit is never given to us in Scripture in isolation from the person and work of Christ or in isolation from the eternal will of the Father. Any endeavor to think of the Spirit in terms that are entirely mystical and divorced from Scripture will take us down all kinds of side streets and eventually to dead ends.

Third, the Holy Spirit was the agent of creation. In the account of creation at the very beginning of the Bible, we are told: "In the beginning, God created the heavens and the earth. The earth was without form and void, and darkness was over the face of the deep. And the Spirit of God was hovering over the face of the waters" (Gen. 1:1–2). The Hebrew word translated as "Spirit" here is *ruach*, which also can mean "breath." The *ruach elohim*, "the Breath of the Almighty," is the agent in creation. It is not the immateriality of the Spirit that is in view here, but rather His power and energy; the picture is of God's energy breathing out creation, as it were, speaking the worlds into existence, putting the stars into space. Thus, when we read Isaiah 40:26 and the question is asked, "Who created these?" we have the answer in Genesis 1:2—the Spirit is the irresistible power by which God accomplishes His purpose.

Tangentially, one of the questions of Old Testament scholarship concerns the extent to which we are able to discover the distinct personhood of God the Holy Spirit from the Old Testament. In other words, can we understand the nature of His hypostasis in the Old Testament alone? When we read Genesis 1, it is not difficult to see that we have in the second verse, certainly in light of all that has subsequently been revealed, a clear and distinct reference to the third person of the Trinity.

In his book *The Holy Spirit*, Sinclair B. Ferguson notes that if we recognize the divine Spirit in Genesis 1:2, that provides what some refer to as the missing link in Genesis 1:26, where God said, "Let us make man in our image." Ferguson observes that this is a clear antecedent reference to the Spirit of God who is at work in Genesis 1:1–2.[3]

This issue reminds us, incidentally, that it is helpful to read our Bibles backward. As we read from the back to the front, we discover the truth of the classic interpretive principle attributed to Augustine: "The New [Testament] is in the Old [Testament] concealed, and the Old is in the New revealed." In other words, we discover the implications of those teachings and events that come earlier in the Scriptures.

Fourth, the Holy Spirit is the agent not only of creation, but also of

God's new creation in Christ. He is the author of the new birth. We see this in John 3, in the classic encounter between Jesus and Nicodemus, where Jesus said, "Truly, truly, I say to you, unless one is born of water and the Spirit, he cannot enter the kingdom of God" (v. 5). This truth, of course, is worked out in the rest of the Scriptures.

Fifth, the Spirit is the author of the Scriptures. Second Timothy 3:16 tells us, "All Scripture is breathed out by God. . . ." The Greek word behind this phrase is *theopneustos*, which means "God-breathed." In creation, we have the Spirit breathing His energy, releasing the power of God in the act of creation. We have the same thing in the act of redemption, and we see it again in the divine act of giving to us the record in the Scriptures themselves. The doctrine of inspiration is entirely related to the work of God the Holy Spirit. Peter affirms this view, writing, "No prophecy was ever produced by the will of man, but men spoke from God as they were carried along by the Holy Spirit" (2 Peter 1:21). The men who wrote the biblical books were not inventing things. Neither were they automatons. They were real people in real historical times with real DNA writing according to their historical settings and their personalities. But the authorship of Scripture was dual. It was, for instance, both Jeremiah and God, because Jeremiah was picked up and carried along. Indeed, in Jeremiah's case, God said, "Behold, I have put my words in your mouth" (1:9). He did so without violating Jeremiah's distinct personality, and he then wrote the very Word of God. This is why we study the Bible— because this is a book that exists as a result of the out-breathing of the Holy Spirit.

Concerning the identity of the Helper, we could go on *ad infinitum*, but we must be selective rather than exhaustive. His identity is as "another Helper." The word translated as "another" here is *allos*, not *heteros*. Jesus promised a Helper of the same kind rather than of a different kind. The Spirit is the *parakletos*, the one who comes alongside. Jesus said He would "be with you forever . . . he dwells with you and will be in you" (John 14:16–17). In other words, His ministry is both permanent and personal.

The Activity of the Helper

What are the active dimensions of the Spirit's work that Jesus introduced? He had much to say, so once again we need to be selective.

First, notice that Jesus said straightforwardly, "When he comes, he will convict the world concerning sin and righteousness and judgment" (John 16:8). What else would a *Holy* Spirit do? How could someone who is intrinsically holy come into an impure world without confronting all of the chaos and sin that is in it?

Some time ago, I was invited to preach in a church where the assigned passage was the account of Jesus cleansing the temple. Part of the challenge lay in addressing the prevailing notion that such action on the part of Jesus was incongruous with a meek and mild Savior

I endeavored to make clear that there was nothing else Christ could do in His searing purity when confronted by all the chaos and exploitation that was represented in that scene. It was His absolute right and authority to confront it. It was a divine necessity to clean the place up, to restore it to the purposes of God. The twelve-year-old Jesus asked Mary and Joseph, "Did you not know that I must be in my Father's house?" (Luke 2:49). When He came back to His Father's house and found that it had become "a den of robbers" (Matt. 21:13), He took action. It was as if He was saying: "It's been eighteen years since I was here, and what a horrible mess you've made of the place. Let's get this cleaned up right now. You merchants and moneychangers—pick your coins up and hit the road. Who do you think you are?"

The next day, the chief priests and elders confronted him and asked, "By what authority are you doing these things, and who gave you this authority?" (Matt. 21:23). Isn't it interesting that they did not challenge what He did? They never said, "Why did You do that?" They were clever enough to know that it was right that He did it, and that they themselves should have done it. He did what needed to be done. But they said, "Do You have any kind of authorization for this?" As John puts it, they asked,

"What sign do you show us for doing these things?" (John 2:18). Jesus said, "Destroy this temple, and in three days I will raise it up" (v. 19). You can just imagine them all putting their wooden heads together to try to figure out what in the world He was saying.

Of course, even the disciples themselves did not comprehend what Jesus meant when He spoke of raising the temple. Later, in fulfillment of Jesus' promise, they understood: "When the Spirit of truth comes, he will guide you into all the truth" (John 16:13).

So the work of the Spirit through Christ and through the followers of Christ is to confront the world, proving the world guilty. The Spirit says: "I will come and prove the world guilty. I will prove it guilty of unbelief. I will prove it guilty of being entirely out of line. I will prove before the plumb line of My absolute holiness and purity that every deviation from it is culpable. I will bring the fact of that guilt home to the lives of individuals."

We have a wee foretaste of this in the Gospel accounts of the crucifixion. Before Jesus died, one of the two criminals crucified beside Him was abusive: "Are you not the Christ? Save yourself and us!" (Luke 23:39). Then the other said: "Do you not fear God, since you are under the same sentence of condemnation? And we indeed justly, for we are receiving the due reward of our deeds; but this man has done nothing wrong" (vv. 40–41). Then, turning to Jesus, he said, "Remember me when you come into your kingdom" (v. 42). What happened there? The Spirit of God confronted the thief in the dying embers of his life with the fact of his unbelief, with the fact that he was out of line, with the fact that he faced the very judgment of God. It makes you want to reach for your hymnal and sing:

I know not how the Spirit moves,
Convincing man of sin,
Revealing Jesus through the Word
Creating faith in him.[4]

Jesus said it was to the disciples' advantage that He should go away and send the Spirit, for this is what the Spirit does. When Pentecost arrived and the Spirit was poured out, Peter—who had had moments of glory and days of disaster—stepped to the fore and gave an amazing historical narrative concerning the nature of God's purposes throughout all of the time of Israel: "This Jesus, delivered up according to the definite plan and foreknowledge of God, you crucified and killed by the hands of lawless men. . . . This Jesus God raised up, and of that we all are witnesses" (Acts 2:23, 32). Being cut to the heart, the crowd called out, "Brothers, what shall we do?" He said, "Repent and be baptized every one of you in the name of Jesus Christ for the forgiveness of your sins, and you will receive the gift of the Holy Spirit" (vv. 37b–38). Immediately, what Jesus had promised in terms of the work of the Holy Spirit was fulfilled.

This is what we see happening in Acts 24, when Governor Felix and his wife, Drusilla, invited Paul to address them. They surely could never have imagined that this prisoner, in all his circumstantial weakness, would speak to them so directly about righteousness, self-control, and the coming judgment. He gave them no soft options; neither did he use the occasion to curry favor or to try to secure his release.

Why did Paul take such an approach? Because he had to—because the world (and their personal world) was guilty, and by the Spirit it needed to be confronted with the fact of its guilt. The world was greedy, selfish, lost, and alone. The world had succumbed to every kind of evil influence and lie. It is no different today, and the idea that preaching the gospel is to offer pablum to people in their predicament, to offer them a blanket, to make them feel a little more comfortable in their horrible circumstances, is a failure to understand what Jesus meant when He said, "It is to your advantage that I go away, for if I do not go away, the Helper will not come to you."

This is the kind of preaching that is largely missing in our day and to which we need to return—preaching that is done in dependence on the Spirit; winsome, but still direct and unequivocal. I fear that some of us may have lost the sense of both the sufficiency of God's Word and the efficacy of God's Spirit, and as a result, our endeavors are increasingly weak and ineffectual.

Second, as I noted above, Jesus told His disciples, "I still have many things to say to you but you cannot bear them now" (John 16:12). When Jesus told them, "This is what the Holy Spirit will do in relationship to the world," the disciples must have said to one another, "I wonder how that is going to happen." So Jesus told them: "When the Spirit of truth comes, he will guide you into all the truth, for he will not speak on his own authority, but whatever he hears he will speak, and he will declare to you the things that are to come" (v. 13). This is an echo of His earlier words: "He will teach you all things and bring to your remembrance all that I have said to you" (John 14:26).

Calvin writes: "But what kind of Spirit did our Savior promise to send? One who should not speak of himself (John 16:13), but suggest and instill the truths which he himself had delivered through the word. Hence the office of the Spirit promised to us, is not to form new and unheard-of revelations, or to coin a new form of doctrine, by which we may be led away from the received doctrine of the gospel, but to seal on our minds the very doctrine which the gospel recommends."[5] In other words, the unique prerogative of the apostles was to be brought into the understanding that they had failed to get, and then, when they had come to an understanding of the truth, under the inspiration of the same Holy Spirit, to write down for us that which we now have in our Bibles so that the truth to which Jesus referred is the truth that, as John Murray puts it, "is deposited in the apostolic witness."[6] Again, this speaks to the absolute necessity of paying close attention to our Bibles.

Third, the activity of the Spirit was to glorify Jesus. Jesus said, "He will glorify me" (John 16:14a). How would He do this? "He will take what is mine and declare it you" (v. 14b). Again, we need to read only into the early chapters of Acts to see this happening. The Spirit of God glorified Christ, both *to* the disciples and *in* the disciples.

Finally, Jesus said: "I will ask the Father, and he will give you another Helper, to be with you forever, even the Spirit of truth. . . . If anyone loves me, he will keep my word, and my Father will love him, and we will come to him and make our home with him" (John 14:16–17a, 23). We become like those with whom we spend time. In the person of the Spirit, the Father and Son came and made Their home with the disciples, and as They did so, the disciples became increasingly like Christ.

The communion to which Christ referred in its unique aspect to the apostles helps us to have a right expectation of our intimate communion with God. Although I know it is often dismissed as an example of superficial piety, the hymn "In the Garden" reminds us of this intimacy: "He walks with me, and He talks with me, and He tells me I am His own."[7] Part of the work of the Spirit is to assure us of our sonship. He comes to us when the Evil One accuses us of our sins, of our failures, of our disconcerting rebellions, and enables us to say, "I know, Father, that You know all of my failings, and that You accept me on Christ's behalf, so I call You Abba, Father, and I thank You that You have come to live with me and in me."

It was vital and beneficial for Jesus to go away. Until that point, He could be in only one place at a time. If He was in Nazareth, He could not be in Bethlehem. If He was in Bethlehem, He could not be in Jerusalem. But His departure and the coming of the Spirit universalized the presence of Jesus, so that He can be in Cleveland and Grand Cayman and China simultaneously. But not only did it universalize the person of Jesus, it internalized the person of Jesus. Until that point, He was with the disciples. He taught them, and though they failed to grasp much of what He said, He was not concerned, because He knew He would send this Comforter, and He would be in the believers. "This," Murray writes, "is the era of the Holy Spirit. I must bring this indictment against the church, that we have dishonoured the Holy Spirit by failing to lay hold of the plenitude of grace and resources which He imparts."[8]

What, then, is the ultimate work of the Spirit of God if not to conform the child of God to the image of the Son of God? How will we know if the Spirit is really fulfilling His purposes in us? We will become increasingly like Jesus. This is God's eternal purpose: "For those whom he foreknew he also predestined to be conformed to the image of his Son" (Rom. 8:29a). This is patently what He is doing: "We all . . . are being transformed into the same image" (2 Cor. 3:18). When the Spirit finishes His work, when Jesus appears, what will we be? "We shall be like him, because we shall see him as he is. And everyone who thus hopes in him purifies himself as he is pure" (1 John 3:2–3). But, of course, that makes perfect sense, because, after all, the Comforter is the Spirit of holiness.

Notes

1 John Calvin, *The Institutes of the Christian Religion*, trans. Henry Beveridge, revised edition (Peabody, Mass.: Hendrickson Publishers, 2008).

2 From the hymn "How Deep the Father's Love for Us" by Stuart Townend, 1995.

3 Sinclair B. Ferguson, *The Holy Spirit* (Downers Grove, Ill.: InterVarsity, 1996), 20–21.

4 From the hymn "I Know Whom I Have Believed" by Daniel W. Whittle, 1883.

5 Calvin, *The Institutes of the Christian Religion*, 1.9.1.

6 John Murray, *Collected Writings of John Murray* (Edinburgh: Banner of Truth, 1982), 3:212.

7 From the hymn "In the Garden" by C. Austin Miles, 1912.

8 Murray, *Collected Writings*, 3:211.

"COSMIC TREASON":

SIN AND THE HOLINESS OF GOD

- Thabiti Anyabwile -

It was Dr. R. C. Sproul who coined the term "cosmic treason" as a synonym for sin. To discover reasons why this term is so appropriate and accurate, we need look no further than Numbers 25, a remarkable passage that gives us a sense of the profound ugliness of sin, especially as it is contrasted with the wondrous beauty of God's holiness. It reads:

> While Israel lived in Shittim, the people began to whore with the daughters of Moab. These invited the people to the sacrifices of their gods, and the people ate and bowed down to their gods. So Israel yoked himself to Baal of Peor. And the anger of the LORD was kindled against Israel. And the LORD said to Moses, "Take all the chiefs of the people and hang them in the sun before the LORD, that the

fierce anger of the LORD may turn away from Israel." And Moses said to the judges of Israel, "Each of you kill those of his men who have yoked themselves to Baal of Peor."

And behold one of the people of Israel came and brought a Midianite woman to his family, in the sight of Moses and in the sight of the whole congregation of the people of Israel, while they were weeping in the entrance of the tent of meeting. When Phinehas the son of Eleazar, son of Aaron the priest, saw it, he rose and left the congregation and took a spear in his hand and went after the man of Israel into the chamber and pierced both of them, the man of Israel and the woman through her belly. Thus the plague on the people of Israel was stopped. Nevertheless, those who died by the plague were twenty-four thousand.

And the LORD said to Moses, "Phinehas the son of Eleazar, son of Aaron the priest, has turned back my wrath from the people of Israel, in that he was jealous with my jealousy among them, so that I did not consume the people of Israel in my jealously. Therefore say, 'Behold, I give to him my covenant of peace, and it shall be to him and to his descendents after him the covenant of a perpetual priesthood, because he was jealous for his God and made atonement for the people of Israel.'"

The name of the slain man of Israel, who was killed with the Midianite woman, was Zimri the son of Salu, chief of a father's house belonging to the Simeonites. And the name of the Midianite woman who was killed was Cozbi the daughter of Zur, who was the tribal head of his father's house in Midian.

And the LORD spoke to Moses saying, "Harass the Midianites and strike them down, for they have harassed you with their wiles, with which they beguiled you in the matter of Peor, and in the matter of Cozbi the daughter of the chief of Midian, their sister, who was killed on the day of the plague on account of Peor."

I want to consider this chapter in four sections, and since I am one of the only Baptist preachers contributing to this book, I had to use alliteration with the outline. The first section (vv. 1–5) is the *horrible context* of this chapter. The second section (vv. 6–9) is the *heightened conflict* caused by man's sin. The third section (vv. 10–13) is the *honorable commendation* that Phinehas receives. The fourth section (vv. 14–18) is the *harrowing condemnation*. In these sections, I will list several observations about sin as cosmic treason.

The Horrible Context

As you know, the events of Numbers 25 occurred following the Exodus, when the Lord God brought His people out of bondage in Egypt. He worked staggering displays of His power in their midst, showing Himself to be the God who delivers His people, a warrior who fights the battles of His people, and a sovereign God who rules over all nations.

When God brought the people to Sinai, He gave them His law, which reminded the Israelites about the heart of His covenant with them. God said, "I am the LORD your God, who brought you out of the land of Egypt, out of the house of slavery" (Ex. 20:2). Then came the commandments: "You shall have no other gods before me" (v. 3) and "You shall not make for yourself a carved image, or any likeness of anything that is in heaven above, or that is in the earth beneath, or that is in the water under the earth. You shall not bow down to them or serve them, for I the LORD your God am a jealous God" (vv. 4–5). These first two commandments are at the heart of the covenant. God pledged to be Israel's God and pledged that they would be His people.

Later, Israel traveled through Moab and ran into a couple of characters—Balaam and Balak (Num. 22–24). Balaam was a prophet for hire, who found that he could not curse God's people, for what God blesses He cannot undo. Balak was a king desperately seeking to put a stumbling block in the way of God's people, fearing what God had done in the life of Israel. The secret hand of God's protection and blessing was hidden from the Israelites' sight. They were not aware of the conversation that was going on between Balaam, Balak, and God. But the God who promised to bless His people was doing just that in preserving and protecting them.

Thus, it is striking when we come to Numbers 25 and see that the Israelites, the people of God, have fallen into sexual immorality and idolatry. The New International Version renders verse 1 this way: "the men began to indulge in sexual immorality with Moabite women." The English Standard Version uses a term that is less polite but more helpful and accurate. It says: "the people began to whore with the daughters of Moab."

That is not language you use in polite company. You don't talk about whores or whoredom. In fact, that is the worst insult that you can assign to a member of the fairer sex. It is not something that you say when you are trying to build a relationship. But have you noticed as you read the Scriptures how often God reaches for this term or for images associated with this term to describe the people of Israel in their sin, rebellion, and treason? Have you read Jeremiah 3 or Ezekiel 16 lately? God does not avoid graphic descriptions of the spiritual adultery of His people.

The physical immorality of the Israelites was only a symptom of their prior spiritual adultery against God. Their treasonous rejection of God preceded their physical bowing before the false gods of Moab. That brings us to the tragically sad verse 3: "So Israel yoked himself to Baal of Peor." We cannot understand the meaning of verse 3 until we view this treason, this desertion, with tears. Israel's loving God had been protecting them from their enemies. Now they were eating and prostrating themselves, whoring themselves with false gods. This is a tragic, horrific, horrible context.

It gets more horrible when we read the second half of verse 3: "And the anger of the LORD was kindled against Israel." I love Matthew Henry's observation at this point. He writes, "We are more endangered by the charms of a smiling world than by the terrors of a frowning world."[1] It was the smiling seduction of the world that ensnared Israel in this idolatry, which in turn called forth God's holy and righteous anger against the sin of His people.

In His anger, God then pronounced a death sentence for all those who participated in this treason: "And the LORD said to Moses, 'Take all the chiefs of the people and hang them in the sun before the LORD, that the fierce anger of the LORD may turn away from Israel'" (v. 4). The language there is a little hard to interpret, but it may be too weak in the English translation. It should be, "Impale them and raise them up on a stick that they might be shown before the nations for the traitors they have been to Me." God was calling for a violent execution.

Moses relayed the instructions: "And Moses said to the judges of Israel, 'Each of you kill those of his men who have yoked themselves to Baal of Peor'" (v. 5). Each leader himself was to carry out the execution of the idolaters. The leaders were not only forbidden to participate in the idolatry but were commanded to personally bring an end to the rebellion. Personally carrying out the sentence would confirm their loyalty. The leaders' hands were to separate their hearts from the treason against God. Carrying out the sentence made them accountable to God's holiness and for the people's holiness.

So this is the horrible context. The holy God, who had been right in the midst of His people, turned to find them lying with another spiritually—worshiping false gods. From this context, I want us to see four ways sin constitutes cosmic treason.

First, sin is a moral evil. It is a negation of what is right. It was good and right for Israel to worship the one true God. But rather than do what was right, they denied this God. They negated what was good, beautiful, and holy. This sin was moral in nature.

This is important because we live in a culture where people often deny any wrongdoing or deny that what they do in the way of sin is wrong. Speak to some folks about their sin and you will hear them say: "It's not sin. It's not wrong. My life is my own. Shouldn't I be able to choose this and to do that?" They deny the sinful quality of sin by establishing their own moral authority contrary to God. That moral authority is reducible to autonomy—self rule. In essence they say, "It is right because I desire it and I don't need anything beyond that as a justification."

We can observe the development of this attitude in our music. Think of the ancient music of the Scriptures, the Psalms. Notice how David responds to his sin in Psalm 51: "Against you, you only, have I sinned" (v. 4). He weeps throughout his psalms about his sin, recognizing it for what it is. Fast-forward several centuries, until we come to Frank Sinatra. He's no David. "Ol' Blue Eyes" tells us, "I did it my way," an anthem to autonomy. One R&B group sang, "If loving you is wrong, I don't want to be right." Today, we have music full of misogynistic content and outright rebellion against God.

We see this moral rebellion in these opening verses of Numbers 25. The people turned to harlots and to idols, doing what they preferred to do rather than what God had called them to do.

Second, sin is rebellion against the rule and the love of God. In the Old Testament, Israel was called God's wife. The people of Israel were known by His name, yet they abandoned Him in adultery. Can you think of a more treasonous act than a wife abandoning her faithful husband and giving herself to another? Can you see how treasonous it would be for such a husband to come home early from work and find his wife engaged with another?

This is only a dim picture of the kind of treason sinners commit against God when they act out their sin nature, when they bow and worship other gods, when they give themselves over to sexual immorality and such. It is treason. It is rebellion of the highest sort. It is the kind of rebellion that seeks to overthrow God Himself.

Third, sin is personal. Sometimes we get the sense in our culture that sin, if people will admit it at all, is something that is not quite right, something that went not as planned, but not something aimed against anyone in particular. We have a sense that our sins are private, that they affect no one. Sin is disembodied and unattached to anything or anyone.

But this passage makes clear, particularly in God's righteous anger and reaction, that sin does land somewhere. Specifically, it lands squarely in the sight of a holy God, who has pledged that He will not look on sin but will judge it in His holiness and righteousness. Sin is committed *against* God Himself. It is falling away from God. It is turning away from God. It is an offense against Him, a very personal attack, a personal rebellion.

Fourth, sin provokes the wrath of an omnipotent God. Again, Henry writes, "Israel's whoredoms did that which all Balaam's enchantments could not do, they set God against them; now he was turned to be their enemy, and fought against them."[2]

I don't know about you, but the scariest thing in the world to me is that people dare to live as if there is no danger associated with sin and God's wrath. False assurance must be the scariest state an unregenerate person can live in. False assurance occurs when people basically think they are OK with God, despite having no saving, covenantal relationship with Him. They delude themselves into thinking that God accepts them even though they live in rebellion. I can't think of a more dangerous situation than that.

Maybe it is a chapter like Numbers 25, where we see a situation of false assurance, that the writer of Hebrews had in mind when he wrote:

> For if we go on sinning deliberately after receiving the knowledge of the truth, there no longer remains a sacrifice for sins, but *a fearful expectation of judgment, and a fury of fire that will consume the adversaries.* Anyone who has set aside the law of Moses *dies without mercy* on the evidence of two or three witnesses. *How much worse punishment,* do you think, will be deserved by the one who has spurned the Son of God and has profaned the blood of the covenant by which he was sanctified, and *has outraged the Spirit of grace?* For we know him who said, "Vengeance is mine; I will repay." And again, "The Lord will judge his people." (Heb. 10:26–30, emphasis added)

In his concluding line, illustrated in Numbers 25, the writer to the Hebrews says, "It is a fearful thing to fall into the hands of the living God" (v. 31).

Do you believe that? Do the non-Christian friends and family members around you believe that? How about the non-Christians in your workplace or in your community, your neighbors? Do you engage them in conversation about spiritual things, about the treasonous nature of sin, as though you are persuaded of the terrors of the Lord, that it is a fearful thing to fall into the hands of the living God?

God is no teddy bear. He is sharp. He has edges. His wrath pierces. His holiness consumes. Those who would commit treason against this God will have this God to deal with on that great day of reckoning. Sin is so treasonous, God pronounced a death penalty against it, as we see in Numbers 25.

The Heightened Conflict

In Numbers 25:4–5, God spoke of the judgment about to fall on those engaging in idolatry and leading others in this treason. When we come to verse 6, we see a startling scene. This verse begins: "And behold." When you see the word *behold* in the Bible, you know what it means: Look. Listen. Pay attention. The verse then goes on: "One of the people of Israel came and brought a Midianite woman to his family, in the sight of Moses, and in the sight of the whole congregation of the people of Israel, while they were weeping in the entrance to the tent of meeting."

Get that picture in your mind, because this is a vivid illustration of the cosmic treason we are talking about. God was speaking to His people. He had summoned them to the tent of meeting, which was where God's people gathered when God wanted to speak with them and speak to Moses, the deliverer. In fiery anger, He had been correcting the treason of His people committed in the plains of Moab. Suddenly, however, this assembly was interrupted and the conflict of the scene was greatly heightened.

Picture, if you will, an Israelite man just outside the congregation. He is holding the hand of a Midianite woman. He sees the people. Some of them are probably bowed, others may be prostrate, and others may have their heads bowed in prayer. But despite seeing this huge gathering of people around the tent of meeting, this man chooses not to join in the covenant worship of God. Can you see him and this Midianite woman sort of stepping over people, working their way through the camp? "Excuse me. Pardon me. Let me get by you here." He did this in the sight of Moses, the lawgiver, and in the sight of the entire congregation while they were weeping at the tent of meeting. That means he did it in the sight of God Himself. He was creeping through the camp with this Midianite woman while the people were weeping over sin just like his. The whores were creeping while the people were weeping.

My mother is the greatest theologian I know. She taught me more about the nature of my sin than any other person on the planet. She started early, too. My mother is normally a very quiet woman. She could beat you to death with silence. But when she spoke, she was plain. She told you where you stood. Sometimes she just basically labeled your wrongdoing. So if you told a lie, for example, she would say: "You know what? You are a lie." But there are degrees of sin. So sometimes my mother would look at you and say, "You are a bald-face lie." I still don't know what "bald-faced" means, but it is worse than just a lie. Then she had a word that indicated you were past the point of no return. She would call you "a brazen lie."

That is what we see as this man walked through the camp with this woman—brazenness. He was not just an idolater. He was not just a bald-faced idolater. This man was brazen in the sight of God and all His holy company. He was walking through the camp thumbing his nose at God.

Phinehas saw this (v. 7). I don't know whether Phinehas did as preachers sometimes do. We're praying, and we look up with one eye to see who is praying along with us. But in some way, Phinehas caught sight of this man. He didn't say a word. He simply got up, picked up his spear, and followed the man into his tent. The assumption here is that Phinehas caught them in the very act of sexual immorality and drove his spear through both of them. He killed the Israelite man and the Midianite woman. But he was not the only one acting at that moment. Verses 8 and 9 tell us that Phinehas' action stopped a plague that God Himself had sent on His people, killing twenty-four thousand Israelites in His holy anger.

Sometimes when you read Scripture, it is very important to pay attention to what you are feeling. Here we read of Phinehas' act and of God killing twenty-four thousand people among the Israelites. Do a self-check. What are you feeling? What is your reaction? We are going to come back to that. But notice that the reaction to sin among God's people was twofold. It was weeping and thrusting. The people wept and grieved over the sin, and Phinehas thrust through the sinner and ended the transgression.

In this section, too, we see some lessons about sin that help us to understand why it is aptly labeled "cosmic treason."

First, the contempt of sin is pictured in the fact that this outrage occurred as the people were assembled before God. This Israelite man brought a Midianite woman to his tent in the sight of everyone. It was contemptuous of him to do so.

Of course, most people don't believe that sin is contempt toward God. We have more polite terms for it. We say, "It was a mistake," or, "I messed up." But at the heart of all sin is a contemptuous attitude toward the person and the work of God, and toward His holiness and righteousness in particular. So next time you're talking with a friend or a family member and you're discussing that person's sin, and he or she starts to use language like "I messed up," just say, "No, I think you have contempt toward God." Do you know what he or she will say? You'll hear something like this: "No I don't! When that happened, I wasn't even thinking about God." When you hear that, just say, "Exactly."

That is the nature of contempt. It is not retaining the knowledge of

God in our lives, in our hearts, and in our affections. It is the suppressing of the knowledge of God, as Paul describes it in Romans 1. We are to be consumed with love for God and the desire to worship Him, but because we're sinners and misshapen in our sin, our contempt for Him manifests itself at the most basic level of not thinking about Him, but delighting in sin. That is why sin is treasonous.

In Genesis 3:15, the Lord promised to put enmity between the seed of the woman—namely Christ, her descendent—and the Serpent. We read quite plainly and helpfully in Romans 8 that the carnal mind, the mind that is set on the flesh, is hostile to God. Somehow the hostility has entered into us, so that we are now contemptuous of God. We are alienated from Him and estranged from Him, and we are at enmity—not with the Serpent but with God. How treasonous! James tells us: "Do you not know that friendship with the world is enmity with God? Therefore whoever wishes to be a friend of the world makes himself an enemy of God" (4:4). Contempt for God is at the heart of this treason.

Second, sin causes us to side with the sinner in his sin before we side with God in His holiness. Earlier, I asked you what you were feeling as we worked through Numbers 25. I suggested you do a self-check and ask: "What am I thinking? What am I feeling? What is going on inside me as I read this rather startling passage of Scripture?" Think back on that. Did you identify with the Israelite man and the Midianite woman, or with Phinehas? Did you have an instinctive and impulsive reaction that drove you to identify with the whores in their whoredom rather than the judge and his javelin? Sin poisons our affections.

When we get down to verse 9, we learn that God had killed twenty-four thousand Israelites by plague. Do you think, "Well, that's an overreaction"? Or do you say, "Yes, vindicate Your name, O God"? Do you side with the sinners in their sin or with God in His holiness? Thanks to the corrupting nature of sin, our loyalty is bent away from the God who made us and owns us to form a pact of loyalty with the sinner and with our sin. It is clear that was happening in Israel, as some of the leaders obviously knew that people were committing spiritual and physical adulteries, yet they didn't act to bring an end to it before God spoke. This treason was deep.

Third, sin leads to our ruin as God puts down our rebellion. The psalmist notes, "The face of the LORD is against those who do evil, to cut off the memory of them from the earth" (Ps. 34:16). Paul writes, "For the wrath of God is revealed from heaven against all ungodliness and unrighteousness of men, who by their unrighteousness suppress the truth" (Rom. 1:18). God is angered by sin; therefore, He judges sin and unrighteousness. Sin leads to our ruin apart from Christ.

Fourth, sin should drive us to weeping and wailing before God because it is such an offense to Him. We should weep like those who were gathered around the tent of meeting. Again the psalmist writes, "The LORD is near to the brokenhearted and saves the crushed in spirit" (Ps. 34:18). The Lord Jesus seems to unpack Psalm 34 as He works His way through the Beatitudes. What does he say? "Blessed are the poor in spirit, for theirs is the kingdom of heaven. Blessed are those who mourn, for they shall be comforted" (Matt. 5:2–3). Then He goes on to this staggering thought: "Blessed are the pure in heart, for they shall see God" (v. 8). The glorious promise of the gospel is that those who weep over their sin, repent in sackcloth and ashes, call upon the mighty name of Christ for deliverance, and rely upon and trust Him will be comforted. Those who are brokenhearted and contrite in spirit will enter the kingdom of heaven. Those who have Christ as their treasure and are joined with Him shall look upon God.

What does the psalmist tell us in Psalm 17:15? "As for me, I shall behold your face in righteousness; when I awake, I shall be satisfied with your likeness." That is the estate Christ has purchased for those who are ruined in sin, but who repent and call on the Lord for His salvation.

The Honorable Commendation

Beginning in verse 10, God spoke again. This time, He spoke to commend Phinehas. He said: "Phinehas the son of Eleazar, son of Aaron the priest, has turned back my wrath from the people of Israel, in that he was jealous with my jealousy among them, so that I did not consume the people of Israel in my jealousy" (v. 11). He then made this promise: "Therefore say, 'Behold, I give to him my covenant of peace, and it shall be to him and to his descendants after him the covenant of a perpetual priesthood, because he was jealous for his God and made atonement for the people of Israel" (vv. 12–13).

Phinehas was a priest in a glorious line; he was a descendent from Aaron and Eleazar. As a priest, it was his job to represent the people before God, to make sacrifices and offerings on the people's behalf, and to represent to the people the holiness of God. That is why he wore a golden plate engraved with the words "Holy to the LORD" (Ex. 28:36). Phinehas understood this calling; this was what prompted him to act against the Israelite man and the Midianite woman. This is what God was commending in him.

God commended Phinehas because he "was zealous with my jealousy." In other words, Phinehas was jealous for God's name in the way God Himself is jealous for His name. So it ought to be with God's people, especially those men who stand behind the sacred desk and shepherd the people of God. The priests were to be the embodiment of the holiness of God. So it is with the Lord's pastors. You might remember the famous quote from Robert Murray McCheyne: "My people have no greater need than the holiness of their pastor."

Likewise, the people were to represent God's holiness to the nations around them. The New Testament tells us that through Christ we have become "a royal priesthood, a holy nation" (1 Peter 2:9). The holiness that was to be placarded on the priest of the Old Testament is now to radiate out of our lives because of the indwelling power and Spirit of Christ.

In chapter 9, R. C. Sproul Jr. makes reference to our brother John Piper, and to the way in which Piper speaks so helpfully about these things. He refers to Piper's main theme: "God is most glorified in us when we are most satisfied in Him."[3] It is a corollary, a related truth, that when God is most glorified and honored, His people are most satisfied. Our satisfaction, our joy, our happiness is bound up together with our God being made known, glorified, loved, celebrated, and embraced.

What else must a priest of God care about than that God would be known? What else must a pastor care about with zeal, with jealously, than that God would be made known and loved for whom He is? What else must the people of God care about than that God, this matchless God, this only God, apart from whom there is no other, would be known, honored, and His fame spread among all the nations? Is not the name of the Lord, the glory of the Lord, the honor of the Lord, the driving impulse among all God's people?

To care *most* about anything *less* than the glory of God is itself treason. To care most about anything other than the supremacy, the glory, and the honor of God is itself treason. It is to abandon God's own agenda for Himself, namely, to be glorified among the nations, and to choose some lesser end than what God Himself has appointed.

Phinehas is not the only one or even the main one to be commended throughout this passage. God Himself must be commended for ending the plague (vv. 9, 11). His anger could have led Him to consume the people, and He would have been right to do so. Yet He ended the plague, accepting Phinehas' action as atonement for the sins of His people. He must be honored for accepting atonement and assuaging His wrath. He also must be honored for loving, glorifying, and vindicating His name (v. 11). There is nothing higher than God; therefore, it is right for Him to love His own name. And He must be honored, praised, and glorified for the covenant that He established with Phinehas, by which He promised Phinehas a perpetual priesthood.

All of these are acts of a gracious God. God is not behaving in this chapter like some petulant child, unwilling to be mollified or satisfied by the toys he is given. No—a thousand no's. God is the sum of all perfections; He is perfect in all of His perfections. His excellencies excel excellence. It is right that He be worshiped, honored, and loved, and so it is right that He act in ways that safeguard His name. All of His actions in this chapter are acts of grace. As we read this, we should commend God. We should praise His name. We should honor Him.

This passage teaches us, first, that because sin is treason, it requires correction. In His holiness, God corrects those whom He loves. He does so, as the writer of Hebrews tells us, so that "we may share his holiness" (12:10). God's love goes hand in hand with His holiness, leading us to participate in that same glorious and wonderful character.

So pastors, do not neglect discipline in your church. Be loving, be patient, be wise. But do not neglect discipline. People, do not bristle at correction. Beware the evidence of treason that resists correction. Resolve now, while you are in your right mind, while you are sober, that if at any point a brother or sister should speak to correct you, you will receive that correction with God's help. You cannot develop holiness of character in a pinch. When sin is sweeping you away, you will not be in your right mind and you will not be inclined to receive the correcting love of God's people. So resolve now in prayer before God, pleading that He would preserve you, and that should you stumble and fall, in the spirit of Galatians 6:1–2, you will receive the correction that God uses as an evidence of His love to restore His people.

Second, because sin is treasonous and because it provokes the righteous anger of God, it requires atonement. God's wrath must be turned away. There must be reconciliation between the sinner and this holy God.

Phinehas' actions were identified with atonement. As a priest, Phinehas points to the Great High Priest, Christ Himself. Phinehas was promised a perpetual priesthood, a promise that was fulfilled in one of his descendents, namely Christ Jesus the Lord. He made the sacrifice that appeased God, but Christ would make the perfect sacrifice that would cleanse God's people of their sin. Phinehas picked up a javelin and speared sinners, bringing about their deaths, but sinners would pierce Christ, whose death would bring life.

Numbers 25 is about the gospel of our Lord, the supremacy of our

Savior, the Lamb of God who takes away the sins of the world, who propitiates, satisfies, and turns away the wrath of God—not for only a moment, not for just a chapter in the Old Testament, but eternally for those who are in Christ. Christ is the true Son of God, the true Priest of God who knew no sin, and yet gave His life as a ransom for sinners.

The Harrowing Condemnation

Finally, notice the way in which the Israelite man and the Midianite woman are remembered: "And the LORD spoke to Moses, saying, "Harass the Midianites and strike them down, for they have harassed you with their wiles, with which they beguiled you in the matter of Peor, and in the matter of Cozbi, the daughter of the chief of Midian, their sister, who was killed on the day of the plague on account of Peor" (vv. 16–18).

The only point at which the Israelite man and the Midianite woman are named is here, in the final verses of this passage. Their names were Zimri and Cozbi (vv. 14–15). Sometimes names become infamously associated with treason. If I were to say to you, "Benedict Arnold," you probably would have a quick and instant understanding that I was referring to someone who was a treasonous rebel. Verses 17–18 identify Zimri and Cozbi as the Benedict Arnolds of the book of Numbers. God called them to account individually for their cosmic treason.

It didn't stop with them—God called the Midianites to account as well, and He used the Israelites as the means of His judgment against the Midianites for their sins (v. 17). This holy God we are talking about is no tribal deity. He is not limited by whether or not the people acknowledge Him. He is God over all. So He exercised His judgment.

Even though you may profess to be a follower of Christ, it may be that you are not a true Christian, that you have not tasted of that saving grace that comes to us through Christ and makes of us new creatures, that joins us to Christ so that we participate in His holiness. In the annals of eternity, do not have it said of you that you were a Zimri or a Cozbi—that you maintained your rebellion against God in sin until God killed you. If you die an unrepentant sinner, you will face God, not the loving, covenant-keeping, gracious God, but the judging God, and you will not stand. The holiness of God in His judgment will be like a consuming fire. It will be indescribable agony. It will be spiritual death, which is so terrible it necessitated the crucifixion of the Son of God. Christ tasted death so that His people would not have to do so.

My non-Christian friend, I plead with you, turn to Christ. Give yourself over to Him. Renounce your sin. Declare war on your sin and call on the name of the Lord, that you might be saved. Call on Christ. Call on Him as Savior, as God. Call on Him as the one who makes atonement for your sins. Trust His sacrifice. Trust His death. Trust His resurrection. Trust His resurrected life as yours. Call on the Lord and the grace of His Spirit that you might be saved and ransomed from sin. There is no life apart from that—only death. Come to Christ and live this day. Blessing and cursing, death and life, are set before you. Choose life. Choose blessing. Call on Christ and be saved in your treason and reconciled to God through Jesus, His Son.

Notes

1 Matthew Henry, *Matthew Henry's Commentary on the Whole Bible* (McLean, Va.: MacDonald Publishing, n.d.), I:687.

2 Ibid.

3 John Piper, *Desiring God: Meditations of a Christian Hedonist* (Sisters, Ore.: Multnomah, 1996), 50.

6

"A HOLY NATION":

THE CHURCH'S
HIGH CALLING

- D. A. Carson -

IN ADDITION TO AN INDIVIDUAL IDENTITY, each of us has a corporate identity. For example, I belong to the group made up of many hundreds who attended the 2009 Ligonier National Conference. We constitute a certain group. Doubtless many among those who attended the conference are Americans. They constitute another corporate identity. Some may be medical doctors, plumbers, or pastors. Some are identified by race, some by a particular ethnicity. Perhaps some belong to the "Fellowship of Motorbike Riders," if there is such a group. These various corporate identities often overlap. Thus, it is quite possible that there is an American who attended the conference and who is also a motorbike rider and a doctor (but perhaps not simultaneously a plumber).

At a merely descriptive level, none of these corporate identities can claim of any sort of precedence over the others. Some people might prefer to think of themselves as bikers first and Americans second, or the reverse. Some might prefer to think of themselves as medical doctors first and African Americans or European Americans second. That's perfectly acceptable. However, our corporate identity as Christians is transcendently important. It outstrips, relativizes, and reduces all other corporate identities.

This truth is hugely emphasized in both testaments. The New Testament does this nowhere more powerfully than in 1 Peter 2, where we read: "But you are a chosen people, a royal priesthood, a holy nation, a people belonging to God, that you may declare the praises of him who called you out of darkness into his wonderful light. Once you were not a people, but now you are the people of God; once you had not received mercy, but now you have received mercy" (vv. 9–10). It will be helpful to follow the flow of Peter's thought in three steps—our identity, our purpose, and then our foundation.

Our Identity as Christians

As he sketches the identity of Christians, Peter first asserts, "You are a chosen people." The word translated here as "people" is sometimes rendered "race." In fact, Peter's language actually makes a specific Old Testament reference, namely, to Isaiah 43:3–4: "I am the LORD your God, the Holy One of Israel, your Savior; I give Egypt for your ransom, Cush and Seba in your stead. Since you are precious and honored in my sight, and because I love you, I will give nations in exchange for you, and peoples in exchange for your life." A little further down in that same chapter, we read:

See, I am doing a new thing! Now it springs up; do you not perceive it? I am making a way in the wilderness and streams in the wasteland. The wild animals honor me, the jackals and the owls, because I provide water in the desert and streams in the wasteland, to give drink to my people, my chosen, the people I formed for myself that they may proclaim my praise. Yet you have not called upon me, O Jacob, you have not wearied yourselves for me, O Israel. You have not brought me sheep for burnt offerings, nor honored me with your sacrifices. I have not burdened you with grain offerings nor wearied you with demands for incense. You have not brought any fragrant calamus for me, or lavished on me the fat of your sacrifices. But you have burdened me with your sins and wearied me with your offenses. I, even I, am he who blots out your transgressions, for my own sake, and remembers your sins no more. (vv. 19–25)

In this passage, God is addressing the people He will rescue from exile in Babylon. They have sinned and fallen into idolatry, but God says He will blot out their sins. They have not offered the appropriate, God-commanded, covenant-stipulated worship. But they remain His chosen people, and therefore He will blot out their transgressions that they may proclaim His praise. Peter picks up this clause in his epistle, as we shall see.

This truth, that the people of Israel are God's chosen, is grounded in the entire matrix of the Old Testament narrative. At the very beginning, Abraham did not volunteer to start a new race; God chose him. In the next generation, not everyone who was descended from Abraham was chosen; it was Isaac, not Ishmael or the packet of progeny from Keturah. In the generation after that, it was Jacob and not Esau. A choice principle was built into God's dealings with Abraham's family from the very beginning. The point is made clear at the national level in Deuteronomy 7 and 10, where God insists that He loves the Israelites not because they are mighty or powerful, or because they are wiser or holier than others, but simply because He set His affection on them. He loves them because He loves them. They are a chosen people, not a choice people.

Peter then applies this language directly to his Christian readers. *They* now constitute the locus of God's chosen people, he says.

People in the Roman Empire in Peter's day were much interested in knowing the class, race, or group to which you belonged. For example, the Roman historian Suetonius, speaking of Christians, writes: "Punishment was inflicted on the Christians, a class." He is writing in Latin, so he uses the word *genus*, which is the Latin equivalent of the Greek word for a race or a group. He goes on to say that the Christians are a *genus* "of men given to a new and mischievous superstition," by which he was referring to the resurrection.

Peter says that believers are "a chosen people," chosen by God from before the foundation of the world, chosen in space/time history, elected in Christ Jesus, and set out as different from all others. But we need to see what immediately precedes this expression. At the end of verse 8, Peter writes that others "stumble because they disobey the message—which is also what they were destined for." Then comes verse 9: "But you are a chosen people. . . ." That's the contrast. It transcends all merely sociological labels, and it identifies Christians as those who, by God's choice and unlike others, obey the message: they submit to the gospel.

Apart from this distinctive, they are an incredibly diverse group. In the very first verse of this epistle, Peter establishes the diversity of his intended first readers: "Peter, an apostle of Jesus Christ, to God's elect, strangers [i.e., exiles] scattered throughout Pontus, Galatia, Cappadocia, Asia and Bithynia." He could have added today: "believers, elect of God, chosen from Vietnam, Kikuyu-speakers from Kenya, those who are gifted in Swahili, some North Americans, and the odd Canadian." They are all there, chosen by God from before the foundation of the world, and for all their diversity, they constitute a separate genus. So Peter first asserts that you are a chosen people.

Second, Peter says, you are "a royal priesthood." Here Peter reaches further back than Babylon. He reaches all the way back to Exodus 19, the chapter that immediately precedes the giving of the Ten Commandments. Here we read: "'Now if you obey me fully and keep my covenant, then out of all nations you will be my treasured possession. Although the whole earth is mine, you will be for me a kingdom of priests and a holy nation.' These are the words you are to speak to the Israelites" (vv. 5–6). The setting, of course, is the exodus, when the Mosaic covenant constituted Israel as God's chosen people, His chosen nation. The crucial expression here could be read as referring to two entities (kingdom and priests) or to one (royal priests). In my judgment, it's the latter.

In the context of the Old Testament, the fact that all the Israelites are royal priests does not mean that there is not also a separate and special category of priests drawn from the tribe of Levi and descended from the line of Aaron. But in the New Testament, the Levitical Aaronic priests foreshadow one of two things. It might be Jesus Christ, our sovereign High Priest, who is the sole Mediator between God and man. This is one of the great themes of the epistle to the Hebrews, and it shows up again in the Pastoral Epistles (see especially 1 Tim. 2:5). There is one Mediator, one go-between, between God and human beings. Alternatively, the priests might foreshadow all believers, as here in 1 Peter. Where that is the case, we're thrown back on the language of Exodus 19.

Therefore, we are forced to ask a question. Since the Old Testament stipulates that there is a special class of priests and you can't volunteer for it—it is by God's sovereign designation of one tribe, that of Levi, and one family, that of Aaron—why does God picture all of His people as priests in Exodus 19?

When we think of priests, there are two lines of thought we should follow. On the one hand, functionally the Old Testament Levitical priests are mediators. They are mediators between a deity—in the pagan world, it could be any kind of deity—and human beings. Under God's self-disclosure, they are mediators who take God's instruction, God's covenantal stipulations, God's ceremonial absolutions, and God's sacrificial system to the people. They present the voice of God, including His demands and His ceremonies, to God's covenant people. Conversely, they take the concerns and the sins of God's people, including their own (for they are fallen men themselves), and bring them before the Lord, discharging the sins with the blood of the covenant, the blood of bulls and goats, shed for the sins of the priest and of the people in the Most Holy Place on the ark of the covenant on Yom Kippur, the Day of Atonement. They are mediators.

This theme is picked up in the New Testament when Paul talks about his evangelism in Romans 15. He says he is discharging his "priestly duty" (v. 16) when he evangelizes. In that sense, Christians are priests not because we have some peculiar clerical role within the church of God, but because, together with all the church of God, we mediate the grace of God to all who are outside. That is what evangelism, in part, is about. Likewise, we pray for those who are outside, that God might open their eyes, that the Spirit of God might convict them of their sin, and that they might repent, turn, and trust the living God. This is part of our priestly ministry. Every time you pray for others, you are engaging in this priestly service. Every time you talk about the gospel with an unconverted neighbor, you are exercising a priestly ministry of mediation.

This notion of "priesthood" has already appeared in 1 Peter. In 2:5, he writes that believers have been built into a spiritual house to be a holy priesthood, offering spiritual sacrifices that are acceptable to God through Jesus Christ. In Hebrews, it is particularly the spiritual sacrifice of praise that is in view (13:15).

All of this has to do with the priests' function. But there is another element. Priests in ancient Israel were especially sanctified, particularly set aside for God. Yet there was a broader sense in which *all* Israelites were set aside for God, God's "royal priests": the focus is not so much on function as on privilege. Likewise, here in 1 Peter, the focus is not so much on the function of mediation as on the reality that all of God's people are to pursue all the sanctification and all the consecration of those who enter as priests into the Most Holy Place, into God's presence. In ancient Israel, under the old covenant, there was a sense in which the average Israelite might say: "Well, the priests have special ablutions to go through and undergo special examination, and only under certain circumstance can they take on the ephod. That's not for me; that is for them alone." God help us when Christians today start saying, "Well, it's all right for the pastor to be holy, but I really don't have to be." All of us are God's priests. All of us have been set aside. All of us have access, now that the veil has been torn, into the very presence of the living God. To start introducing a double-tier standard of holiness or of consecration makes no sense this side of the cross and resurrection of the Lord Jesus.

This emphasis on the sheer privilege of being sanctified, of being set aside as God's special people, is introduced by Peter in his opening verses: "Peter, an apostle of Jesus Christ, to God's elect, exiles spread throughout Pontus, Galicia, Cappadocia, Asia and Bithynia, who have been chosen according to the foreknowledge of God the Father, through the sanctifying work of the Spirit, for obedience to Jesus Christ and sprinkling with his blood: Grace and peace be yours in abundance" (1:1–2). You are a royal priesthood, a priesthood that serves the King of the universe.

Third, Peter says you are "a holy nation." This idea also is grounded in Exodus 19. God says, "Although the whole earth is mine, you will be for me a kingdom of priests *and a holy nation*" (Ex. 19:5b–6a, emphasis added). The contemporary notion of nation—the "nation-state" as we think of it in the Western world—is an eighteenth-century creation. The word translated "nation" here is the word that actually produces our English word *ethnicity*. You might render this: "you are a holy ethnicity" (although that sounds just a bit too narrowly racial for some of us).

I was brought up in French Canada. French Canadians would speak of "*la nation du Quebec*"—the nation of Quebec. But the word *nation* in French means something a little different from *nation* in English. In English, it is a geographical political entity. But in the ancient world, although there were geographical political entities, they tended to be regional empires or the like, and then under the regional empires there were tribes or ethnicities with various associations and self-identities. In French Canada, something of this old flavor is there. Although French Canadians know that nationally in the English sense they are Canadians, nevertheless, nationally in the French sense, they are French Canadians and quite proud of it. To English ears, hearing French Canadians say that they belong to the nation of Quebec sounds like an insult to the rest of Canada, as if somehow they are distancing themselves from Canada. But that is not quite what most French Canadians mean. They are simply saying they belong to the ethnicity of francophone Canadians.

What kind of ethnicity do we belong to? What is our nation? Peter says "you are . . . a holy nation." What does that mean?

The categories of systematic theology have long distinguished between the communicable attributes of God—that is, the attributes of God that He may share with non-God image-bearers like you and me—and the non-communicable attributes of God, that is, the attributes of God that He cannot share with image-bearers like us. Thus, there is no biblical passage that says "be omnipotent, for I am omnipotent." Let's face it, omnipotence is an incommunicable attribute of God. On the other hand, there are many passages that enjoin us to love. God is love, and love is a communicable attribute of God. It is one of His attributes that can be shared between Him and His non-God image-bearers.

Where does holiness fit into this? It is an extraordinary category. On the one hand, it is a communicable attribute. After all, God says, "Be holy, because I am holy" (Lev. 11:44). That puts it on the communicable attribute side. But as you work through the uses of the word *holy* in the Bible, you discover that it has concentric rings of meaning. What exactly does it mean to be holy?

Some try to deal with the term in etymological categories. That is, they try to break it down into its components, as they perceive them. They note that *holy* means "separate" and they point out that God is utterly separate. But did the voices around the throne in Isaiah 6:3 really cry, "Separate, separate, separate is the LORD Almighty"? The word *holy* loses something when it is defined this way. Others want the term to have an overtone of morality. But did the voices around the throne really say, "Moral, moral, moral is the LORD Almighty"? No. At its core, in the tightest concentric circle, *holy* is almost an adjective for God. God is

God; God is holy, and even angels of the highest order cover their faces with their wings as they join in the paeans of praise of the heavenly hosts and cry, "You are God, You are God, You are God. Holy, holy, holy is the LORD Almighty." I cannot get closer to the word than that.

Then, as you stretch out a little further, that which peculiarly belongs to this God is said to be holy. It may or may not be moral. For example, the shovel that takes the ash from the altar is said to be holy (Num. 4:14–15), but not because it is moral. A shovel is never moral. The shovel is holy because it is reserved exclusively for God's service and work. Anything else is common and therefore profane. So the shovel is said to be holy. The shovel is not itself God, but it belongs exclusively to God. Then, of course, if the belonging refers not to a shovel but to people, the manner in which we belong to God affects how we think, how we behave, what we say, and our relationships. For we have the potential to reflect something of the character of God in ways that shovels don't have. If we human beings are holy, inevitably a moral overtone creeps into the notion in a way it cannot do when that which is holy is a shovel.

This holiness of God's people is sometimes definitional. We are set apart for God, and thus we are sanctified, holy. We are holy by the very fact that we have been set apart by God (so Paul says of the Corinthians in 1 Cor. 1:2). If we are set apart by God and then do not live like it, we besmirch the holiness of God. We betray what we are. We contradict the very essence of what God has called us to be. Thus, sometimes this holiness is behavioral. If we are definitionally His, and the pleasure, privilege, and power of being His work out in our lives behaviorally, then we become holy at a kind of functional level, too.

To tell the truth, the word *holy* can actually extend in a concentric circle even farther out than this. In a handful of passages in the Old Testament, the term *holy men* is used to refer even to pagan priests—not because they are holy in the narrow concentric circle senses, but because they are operating in the domain of the sacred. They are not merely secularists. They are not merely tied to matter. Transparently, then, the range of the holiness word-group is very broad, and the individual context holds the key to understanding each occurrence.

At its core, then, I am sorely tempted to say that holiness in an incommunicable attribute of God. I am not quite happy to say that. But it's very close. Only God is God; only God, in the ultimate sense, is holy. But the entailments of His holiness wash out in concentric waves. We are to belong to Him and be His holy nation, peculiarly His, such that God in His infinite mercy dares call us holy—a holy people, a holy ethnicity, a holy nation. Thus, holiness becomes a communicable attribute of God.

Inevitably, if this really is our self-identity and we understand it as such, we will experience conflicts with our other corporate identities, whether as Americans, females, whites, Chinese, or motorbike riders. There will be overlaps of blessing that come from common grace, but there will be conflicts. How we resolve them will turn largely on whether or not, in God's grace, these categories that form our identities are of great importance for us. For they should not, not ever, run competition with what it means to us to belong to this blood-bought holy ethnicity, God's holy nation.

Fourth, Peter writes, you are "a people belonging to God." Again, this is grounded in Exodus 19. As we have seen, God says, "Although the whole earth is mine, you will be for me a kingdom of priests and a holy nation" (Ex. 19:5b–6a).

What does this mean? We must never think that we are a people belonging to God, God's possession, in some sense that disqualifies God from claiming possession of everyone and everything else, of every other nation and entity, of everything in the entire universe. There is a range of meaning in passages that speak of God's possessions. In one sense, God possesses everything He made, which is the point of the concessive clause ("Although the whole earth is mine"); in another sense, He has chosen Israel to be His special possession, peculiarly His people.

We find exactly the same kind of range of uses when it comes to the kingdom. In one sense, God's kingdom is God's dynamic reign. It is virtually co-extensive with what we mean when we refer to His sovereignty.

We are told by the psalmist, "His kingdom rules over all" (Ps. 103:19). In that sense, you are in the kingdom whether you like it or not. You cannot escape from that kingdom. No nation, no ethnicity, can ever escape from this God. He made it all and He possesses it all. There is a sense in which the Iranian ethnicity is owned by God. The Kamba ethnicity, in eastern Africa, is owned by God. There is no ethnicity that is not owned by God: no nation, no people, no planet, no universe. Some scientists are talking about multiple universes. I've got enough on my hands trying to understand this one rather than multiplying endless theoretical ones, but however many there are, they are all owned by God.

Yet *kingdom* can have a variety of more restricted usages, including, for example, what Jesus says in John 3—only those who are born again from above belong to, can see, and can enter the kingdom of God. In that sense, the kingdom is that subset of all of God's sovereignty under which there is eternal life. You may or may not be in the kingdom in that sense.

Similarly, there is a range of referents in an expression such as "God's possession" or "a people belonging to God." Israel is God's unique special possession. This is a spectacular notion. It should instill in us awe, wonder, and a sense of privilege, especially when we perceive that this status is by His initiative, by His choice, by His doing. That language is picked up by the apostle Peter. He understands that what is said of God's covenant people under the terms of the old covenant is exactly what must be said of God's covenant people under the terms of the new. The church is God's special possession, a people belonging to God.

So what does Peter say to establish our corporate identity? He says, in effect, "You are a chosen people; a royal priesthood; a holy ethnicity—a holy nation; God's special possession."

I hope you now see that these categories are not discreet, hermetically sealed-off things that are added to one another. They overlap. In each case, there is an emphasis on God's initiative, on supreme God-centeredness, and on the built-in implication of incalculable privilege over against every other form of self-identity. We are God's people, sanctified by God, chosen by God, loved by God. We are His priesthood, His nation, His people. This is our identity.

Our Purpose as Christians

Come back to 1 Peter 2:9: "But you are a chosen people, a royal priesthood, a holy nation, a people belonging to God, *that you may declare the praises of him who called you out of darkness into his wonderful light*" (emphasis added). The language is drawn from Isaiah 43:20–21. There God says, "I provide water in the wilderness and streams in the wasteland, to give drink to my people, my chosen, the people I formed for myself that they may proclaim my praise." Peter follows the exact language of the Septuagint, the Greek translation of the Old Testament. There it is recorded that the reason believers enjoy this corporate identity is to show "the praises [or "the excellencies"] of him who called you out of darkness"—either "praises" or "excellencies" is acceptable. It is either the praise itself or the ground for the praise (the excellencies of God); it makes very little difference in terms of the outcome. The point is that we have received all of these privileges in order that we may declare the praises or excellencies of Him who called us out of darkness into His wonderful light. In other words, all of our special status, all of our corporate identity as the people of God, the church of the living God, is not to promote pride or a sense of intrinsic superiority, still less, God help us, one-upmanship with respect to other religions or other races. Rather, it is that we might declare the excellencies of Him who called us out of darkness into His wonderful light.

Two details in this line are crucial. First, there is the sheer God-centeredness of this purpose. I have been doing university missions off and on for about thirty-five years. About a dozen years ago, I started stumbling across a question from university undergraduates that I never received when I was a young man. This relatively recent question is put variously, but it generally runs something like this: "Amongst human beings, anyone who wants to have all of the attention and garner all the praise, anyone who wants to be the focus of everyone's constant admiration, with everyone stroking that person and fawning all over him, would be thought of as massively egocentric. The God you are trying to push on us looks to me to be very egocentric. He keeps demanding that we praise Him all the time. For goodness sake, is He insecure? Isn't He, at very least, morally defective?"

What do you say to that? The reason I never heard that sort of question in the past, I suspect, is because until fairly recently most of the unconverted people I met in university missions had been brought up in the Judeo-Christian heritage, which held that there is a sovereign, transcendent God, and that He is unique and deserves special attention. But now things have changed. Thirty years ago, if I were dealing with an atheist, at least he or she was a "Christian atheist." That is, the God he or she disbelieved in was the Christian God, which is another way of saying that the categories were on my turf. But I can't assume that now.

So it's difficult to respond. Of course it's true to say something like this: "Yes, but God is so much more than we are. He's not just another human being, slightly 'souped-up.' He is God. He is the Creator. He is to be cherished and revered. He is our Maker and our Sovereign and our providential King and our Judge." All of that is true.

But there is more. It is one of the themes John Piper likes to preach about. It is this: Because we have been made by this God and for this God, because our very self-identity when we are right with God is to love Him supremely, to adore Him and to worship Him, it is a supreme act of love on His part to keep demanding it—because it is for our good. What conceivable good would it do for us if God were to say: "Don't give Me too much worship. I'm just One of you guys. Slightly ratchet it up maybe, but don't focus on Me too much." That might satisfy some idolater's notion of humility, but the humility that I see in this King of kings is on Golgotha. That He keeps directing attention to Himself is an act of supreme humility and grace, precisely because He stoops to remind us of what we ought to recognize, and because it is for our good.

There is no insecurity in this God. After all, He is the God of aseity. He has no needs. In eternity past, the Father loved the Son, the Son loved the Father, and They were perfectly content. God is not demanding that we love Him so that we can meet the needs of His psychological profile this week. His focus on Himself is not only because He is God, but because, out of love, that is what we need. That is what we must see. That is the point to which our adoration must come. If it does not, we wallow in idolatry again and again and again.

But there is a second detail in this purpose clause of singing His excellencies. Not only is there the sheer God-centeredness of our purpose, there is the sense of sheer privilege in this purpose when we see what He has done. We are His chosen people, His royal priesthood, and so forth, so that we may declare the praises of Him who called us out of darkness into His wonderful light. Now we are tied into the Bible's storyline. We are the people who shook our puny fists in God's face in Eden. We are the people who rightly stand under the curse. We are alienated from God, without hope, to use Paul's language (Eph. 2:12). We are by nature objects of wrath (Eph. 2:3). We are in darkness without purity, cut off, but calling it freedom even though it spells death. But God has rescued us from this darkness and brought us into wonderful light (1 Peter 2:9). What a privilege is ours to sing His praises.

Our Foundation as Christians

Peter continues, "Once you were not a people, but now you are the people of God; once you had not received mercy, but now you have received mercy" (2:10). The language is again tied to the Old Testament, this time to the prophet Hosea. I want to look at several verses in Hosea 1 and 2 that are very important if we are to understand Romans 9 and 1 Peter 2 on the grafting of Gentiles into God's covenant.

You will recall the burden of the prophet Hosea. He is commanded to marry Gomer, who is a betrayer from the beginning, an adulteress. Hosea learns something of what God feels in Himself as the Almighty cuckold— the betrayed husband. We read the consequence of this in Hosea 1:6–7:

> Gomer conceived again and gave birth to a daughter. Then the LORD said to Hosea, "Call her Lo-Ruhamah [which means "not loved"], for I will no longer show love to the house of Israel, that I should at all forgive them. Yet I will show love to the house of Judah; and I will save them—not by bow, sword or battle, or by horses and horseman, but by the LORD their God." After she had weaned Lo-Ruhamah, Gomer had another son. Then the LORD said, "Call him Lo-Ammi [which means "not my people"], for you are not my people, and I am not your God."

But at the end of chapter 2, this same God who has rejected them talks about how He will take this people back to the land. He says in verse 23: "I will plant her for myself in the land; I will show my love to the one I called 'Not my loved one.' I will say to those called 'Not my people,' 'You are my people'; and they will say, 'You are my God.'" In the context of Hosea, you cannot help but see that those who are declared by God not to be loved and not to be His people are all Israelites. Then, to those Israelites who have been, in effect, excommunicated, God in His mercy reaches out and says, "You are my people and I am your God."

Now we come to the way these verses are quoted both by Paul in Romans 9:25 and by Peter in 1 Peter 2. In both passages, Paul and Peter extend what Hosea said. They take God's clear reference to the Israelites, who were declared not to be God's people but then were declared to be God's people again, and extend it to Gentiles, who were not God's people and are now declared to be God's people. This, it has to be said, has made a lot of commentators very upset, because it seems to them that Paul and Peter are ripping the text out of its context.

But the point both Paul and Peter are making is in fact profound. The point is that once Israel has been judicially declared by God to be "not my people," they are indistinguishable from the pagans. They really are not His people. It is a judicial sentence. That is exactly Paul's argument in Romans 1:18–3:20. Romans 3:21 opens up one of the greatest atonement passages in all of Holy Writ. But in the two and a half chapters before that, Paul's point is that Jew and Gentile alike are closed up under sin. We are all a damned breed. We are all lost. There is no hope for any of us. It doesn't matter if we were under the Mosaic covenant or not. We are all sinners. That is the point.

Because Israel itself has become "not my people," if God reaches down in His sovereign grace and reaches those who are not His people and says, "You are my people," it doesn't really matter whether He speaks this way to those who are ethnically Israelites or those who are ethnically anything else. They are all damned. They are all lost. They are all not His people. It is by God's sovereign, gracious reaching out that He takes, saves, transforms, and makes those who were not His people into His people.

That's what is going on here in 1 Peter 2. Peter writes, "Once you were not a people" (v. 10a). He does not distinguish; he does not write to the half of the church that is Gentile and say, "Once you Gentiles were not his people." The whole lot, the whole mixed-race church, Jews and Gentiles, were all not God's people. How can he say anything else? Paul likewise says that we were all by nature objects of wrath (Eph. 2:3); we were all lost, all justly condemned, all not His people.

Peter goes on, "But now you are the people of God; once you had not received mercy, but now you have received mercy" (v. 10b). At this juncture, we are called to remember once more the opening verses of the first chapter, which anticipate the contrast: "To God's elect, *strangers [exiles]* scattered throughout the provinces of Pontus, Galatia, Cappadocia, Asia and Bithynia, *who have been chosen according to the foreknowledge of God the Father, through the sanctifying work of the Spirit, to be obedient to Jesus Christ and sprinkled with his blood*" (vv. 1b–2a, emphasis added). Likewise, he writes in 1 Peter 2:24–25: "'He himself bore our sins' in his body on the tree, so that we might die to sins and live for righteousness; 'by his wounds you have been healed.' For 'you were like sheep going astray,' but now you have returned to the Shepherd and Overseer of your souls." To put these contrasts in other words, we who had not received mercy have now received mercy.

Everything that we enjoy as God's chosen possession, as God's royal priesthood, as God's holy ethnicity has been secured by the cross, by the sprinkled blood. The forgiveness that gives us reconciliation to this living God is secured by the cross, because He bore our sins in His own body on the tree. The Holy Spirit, who has been poured out on us to bring us conviction of sin and sanctifying power, is secured by the cross. Once you were not a people; the cross made you a people. Once you had not received mercy; by the cross the mercy of God has been poured out on you.

So our identity, our purpose, and our foundation all are tied to the cross. Once our self-identity is established corporately in these terms, once we think of ourselves as "the church of the living God" in these terms, there is an end to racism. There is an end to nationalism. It's not that there is no place left for being thankful for a certain "natural" heritage, but everything is now relativized under the glory of belonging to the people of the eternal God. We are blood-bought, secured by an anchor in God's sovereign purposes from eternity past and given a prospect before us into eternity future, a resurrection existence in a new heaven and a new earth.

From darkness into light, from "no mercy" to mercy, from "not God's people" to "God's people." Such an identity is not established by banging a drum, declaring we are Christians, preaching unity as an end in itself, and singing "Kum Ba Yah." It is grounded in what God has done in Christ Jesus, and as a result, we become, so help us God, so God-obsessed, so Christ-obsessed, so cross-obsessed, so truth-of-the-gospel-obsessed that all of our diversities, all of our other corporate identities, however pleasurable, ephemeral, attractive, or interesting they may be, though in any other framework they may serve to push us apart, now become part of the spectrum that brings glory to our Creator and Redeemer—this holy diversity in the church of the living God.

7

"WOUNDED FOR OUR TRANSGRESSIONS":

THE HOLINESS OF GOD AND THE CROSS

- W. Robert Godfrey -

CAN YOU REMEMBER A SINGLE SENTENCE THAT ANY of your professors ever spoke to you? I don't remember many, but I can remember one sentence from a rather liberal theologian, Robert McAfee Brown. He once said in class: "This is the essence of American religion—I like sinning and God likes forgiving, and the world is well put together." That statement has stayed with me over the decades. I am afraid he was right—that does tend to be the American attitude.

The tragedy of this attitude is that it trivializes everything. It turns me into a naughty grammar-school kid and God into an indulgent grandfather who thinks we are kind of cute in our naughtiness. But more than a trivialization, this view is a profound lie. It is a complete misrepresentation of who we are, of what sin is really all about, and most important, of whom God is. John Calvin begins his *Institutes of the Christian Religion* by saying, "Nearly all the wisdom we possess, that is to say, true and sound wisdom, consists of two parts: the knowledge of God and of ourselves."[1] If we do not know God and we do not know ourselves, we really do not know anything accurately. Therefore, if we think sin is just slightly dysfunctional behavior and God is an indulgent grandfather in heaven, we have a false understanding of reality and life.

In this chapter, I want us to dig into the Scriptures to regain some sense of the holiness of God, the sinfulness of man, and the seriousness of salvation. I can think of no better place to start than with Isaiah 6, but I want to approach this chapter from a somewhat unusual angle.

Why King Uzziah's Death Matters

Isaiah 6 begins with the words, "In the year that King Uzziah died I saw the Lord . . ." (6:1a). I think most of us rush right past that opening phrase; I did so for many years. Many commentators treat it just as a date, a calendar mark. Uzziah died early in Isaiah's ministry, so many commentators conclude that Isaiah is making the point that he had this vision early in his ministry. That certainly is part of what Isaiah intends. Others perceive a kind of causal relationship here. I vividly remember going to church the Sunday after President Kennedy was assassinated and hearing the minister preach from this text: "In the year that King Uzziah died I saw the Lord." He said the death of great men is an occasion for reflection and an opportunity to see God. That also is true, but I do not think Isaiah is saying that the death of the king somehow prompted his vision of God.

I think our understanding of Isaiah 6 and, as we move on, Isaiah 53 will be deepened greatly if we pause for a moment to think about the reign of King Uzziah. Confession is good for the soul, so I must tell you that when I began studying this topic and thought about the reign of King Uzziah, I could not remember anything about it. However, we can read about Uzziah and his reign as king of Judah in 2 Chronicles 26. There we find Uzziah described as a good monarch. Every account of the reign of one of the kings of Israel or Judah in the books of Kings and Chronicles seems to begin with a sort of summary statement that not only describes the beginning of the reign but gives an evaluation of the whole reign. So 2 Chronicles 26 tells us that Uzziah was a good king as kings go. He reigned fifty-two years and accomplished wonderful things—he built cities, he conquered enemies, and he encouraged technological development of his military. Meanwhile, the wealth and herds of his people increased. He was a good "guns-and-butter" king. He seemed to live out the meaning of his name in Hebrew: "The Lord is my strength." We are told that the Lord gave him success. The Lord prospered him and helped him.

After all of that success, all of that accomplishment, and all of that blessing, however, Uzziah became proud. Uzziah repeated the history of God's people throughout the Old Testament. When they suffered, they complained. When they were prosperous, they forgot God. Uzziah prospered and forgot that all he had was from the hand of the Lord and that all he had accomplished was by the Lord's blessing. Thus, he became proud. Interestingly, the Hebrew word translated as "proud" in our English Bibles means "lifted up." Uzziah became "lifted up." He lifted himself up in his own heart, saying, "I'm really something, aren't I?" In short, he became corrupt and faithless.

The Bible does not leave us with just this general picture of the problems of Uzziah's pride. We are given an account of a remarkable and horrifying incident that illustrates how "lifted up" he was. He seems to have surveyed the nations around him and discovered that all the kings of those nations were priest-kings. They not only ruled the civil affairs of their lands, they also ministered as priests in the temples. This meant that all power, civil *and* religious, was concentrated in their hands. Uzziah thought: "Someone as important, as great, as noble, and as successful as I should be like these other kings. I, too, should be a priest-king. Why should the Holy Place in the temple be off-limits to me? Am I not as great as the other kings? Am I not at least as great as my neighbors to the north, the kings of Israel?" We read that early in his reign, Jeroboam, the first ruler of the northern kingdom of Israel, burned incense before the Lord on the altar he had set up in Bethel (1 Kings 13). He functioned as a priest-king. So Uzziah said, "If it was good enough for Jeroboam, it is good enough for me." He wanted to follow the example of the kings of Israel, every one of whom is described in Scripture as evil.

Therefore, in his pride, he marched into the sanctuary of God to burn incense. But as he marched, the priests surrounded him and said, "Don't do it, don't do it, don't do it." He would not be deterred; he wanted to be a priest-king. So there in the Holy Place, in that moment, the Lord struck him with leprosy. The priests rushed him out of the sanctuary. Afterward, we are told, he lived in a "separate house," presumably a palace, for the rest of his life, cut off from the house of the Lord. When he died, they buried him with the kings, and they said, "He is a leper." That was his epitaph. Not "He *was* a leper" but "He *is* a leper." That was all there was to say about him. The Scriptures are willing to say that, on balance, Uzziah was a good king, but at the heart of his reign was this terrible sacrilege.

A Vision of the True King

With that background in mind, let us go back to Isaiah 6: "In the year that King Uzziah died I saw the Lord sitting upon a throne, high and lifted up" (v. 1a). The same word used of Uzziah is used here of God when Isaiah says He was "lifted up." Isaiah suddenly sees the true King of Israel on His throne in the sanctuary, exalted among His people, glorious. It is as if Isaiah is saying to us, "Think of the contrast between this exalted God and poor little pretentious Uzziah."

Isaiah also notes, "and the train of his robe filled the temple" (v. 1b). I have always enjoyed watching royal weddings. Perhaps I am a monarchist at heart. One of the things that is always impressive is the trains. Usually the broadcasters provide an overhead view of the royals going down the aisle with their long trains, and some of the trains are so long and so heavy that the royals have trainbearers. If the trainbearers were to drop the train, the royal would be stopped in his or her tracks because it is too heavy to move. But our God is so glorious that His train can fill the temple and it does not slow Him down a bit. It does not hinder Him in any way. This massive train points to the glory of this King in His temple.

Isaiah continues, "Above him stood the seraphim" (v. 2a). The word *seraphim* is derived from the word for "burning." I think it really has to do with the rays of the sun. Yet these rays of sunlight that surround the throne and the temple are insignificant in their glory and brightness compared to the Lord Himself. So these angels fly and speak one at a time, saying, "Holy, holy, holy is the Lord of hosts" (v. 3a). They add, "The whole *earth* is full of his glory!" (v. 3b, emphasis added). The temple is a concentration point of God's presence in the earth. It declares that the glory of God seen by Isaiah in this sanctuary is in fact the glory of a God, a King who reigns over the whole earth and is majestic in His holiness.

The majesty of this King is so great that the building shakes at the sound of the praise (v. 4a). My wife used to be a high school teacher in the public schools. We had to chaperone a dance when we were young. I remember standing in the gym where the dance was held and feeling my collarbone vibrate to the rock music. It was that loud. Well, the music in Isaiah's vision shakes the very building in its glory.

Furthermore, Isaiah says, "the house was filled with smoke" (v. 4b). Why is the temple filled with smoke? The Scriptures frequently refer to smoke surrounding the Lord. We could think of Psalm 97:2, for example: "Clouds and thick darkness are all around him; righteousness and justice are the foundation of his throne." Or we could think of Revelation 15:8: "the sanctuary was filled with smoke from the glory of God and from his power, and no one could enter the sanctuary until the seven plagues of the seven angels were finished." Smoke is a mark of the glory of God. It is a mark, in a sense, of the hiddeness of God, the inapproachability of God, our inability to see God as He is in Himself.

More than that, I think there is also an allusion here to the smoke that rises from the altar of incense before the Lord. In the Old Testament temple, the altar of incense stood right before the veil, and it symbolized the prayers of God's people going up before Him. In other words, it symbolized the essence of the temple as the place where God met with His people. The holy God came and heard the purified prayers of His people rising as the smoke from the altar of incense rose. This is a picture of the connection of God and His people. I think this smoke, in part, reminds us that those incense fires are burning, and that beautiful aroma and smoke rises to fill the sanctuary and surround God with the praises of all His people. The smoke Isaiah saw is a picture of this blessed fellowship.

Then we begin to see how profound was the desecration Uzziah committed, to come into this place and corrupt it, to mar its holiness. One of the chores of studying the Old Testament is to read those seemingly endless chapters that tell us all about the exact construction of the temple, the exact ceremonies that were held there, and all the details of the clergy. When we read these passages, we are a little inclined to think, "Let's get on with it." But every one of those details says to us that God is holy and pure, and that we cannot simply saunter into His presence. The temple is the great children's picture book of the Old Testament, speaking about how pure God is and how serious He is about His purity, and what cost there is for sinners to be able to enter into His holy presence. Every detail is a reminder to us that we have no proper instincts about worship.

Calvin warned against seeking to please ourselves rather than God in our worship: "Nor can it be doubted but that, under the pretense of holy zeal, superstitious men give way to the indulgences of the flesh."[2] The Old Testament descriptions of the temple are God's way of constantly saying to us: "Be aware. Be aware. Be aware of how serious the Lord is about meeting with us." We need to remember Aaron's sons, who offered strange fire on the altar of incense and were struck dead then and there (Lev. 10). That's how serious the Lord is. He is not an indulgent grandfather.

From Holiness to Sinfulness

So we see a picture of the holiness of God here in Isaiah's vision of God in the temple. We also see a picture of the sinfulness of man. Isaiah says, "Woe is me!" (v. 5a). He gets it. He is overwhelmed. He is humbled. He does not say, "I have every right to be here," or, "I belong in the sanctuary." He is overwhelmed with a sense of his unworthiness as he sees the holiness of God.

He goes on: "I am a man of unclean lips" (6:5b). Do you know what the lepers had to cry when they walked through the streets in the ancient world, to warn people that they were coming, so that people could get out of the way so as to avoid any contact with leprosy? They had to cry, "Unclean." I think that Isaiah hears the seraphim declaring the glory of God and praising His holiness, and he thinks of Uzziah just dead and buried, and that epitaph, "He is a leper." I think Isaiah is saying: "Woe is me, I am undone, for I am a leper. My lips are leprous. I cannot praise God. I cannot enter His presence, because I am a leper. I am unclean."

Now this word *unclean* does not necessarily mean leprosy. It can mean other kinds of ritual and moral corruption as well. But I think leprosy is part of what Isaiah has in mind here. Thinking of Uzziah, he is overwhelmed with the sense of leprosy as a sign and symbol of the sinfulness of the people and of the corrupting effects of sin. Leprosy was a terrible disease as it progressed. It destroyed nerves and left the victim numb and increasingly visibly deformed. Because of the numbness, rats could chew a victim's fingers off as he slept and he would not feel it. These symptoms illustrate the horror of this disease, which left its victim increasingly weakened, deformed, and corrupted, and therefore increasingly shunned by mankind. In all these ways, the victim of leprosy was seen to be stricken by God, as Leviticus says over and over again of those who are lepers.

This is how Isaiah is analyzing his sinful condition before the Lord. It is as if he is saying: "Suddenly I see and know, Lord, that it is not just Uzziah who was a leper, but I am a leper. My people and I are leprous in our pride, in our failure to listen to Your Word, in our failure to follow You faithfully. O Lord, woe unto us. We are undone. We are ruined."

I do not think it is unimportant that Scripture records that leprosy broke out on Uzziah's forehead. The high priest, when he entered the temple, was to wear some kind of headdress such as a mitre or a turban. From that headdress was to hang a signet stone, and on that signet was to be inscribed the words "Holy to the Lord." The priest who ministered to God at the altar was to come there, at least symbolically, clothed in holiness. But Uzziah came in corruption of heart, and he then was visited with the evidence of that corruption, beginning on his own forehead. God was saying, in effect: "How dare you, Uzziah? You are no priest-king. How dare you desecrate the house of the Lord?" With a sense of what that picture of Uzziah's suffering meant for the people of God, Isaiah cries: "Woe is me. I am undone. I am unclean. I am a man of unclean lips."

What does Isaiah do then? Does he say, "I will take myself in hand and improve myself"? No. There is nothing he can do. He recognizes his helplessness in sin, just the way an ancient leper was helpless in his disease. There was nothing a leper could do to help himself. There was nothing Isaiah could do to help himself.

The God Who Comes to Lepers

So we move on to a picture of salvation, a picture of God's action, for that is what salvation is. Lepers can be helped only by a God who will come to them, and that is what we see in Isaiah 6:6: "Then one of the seraphim flew to me, having in his hand a burning coal that he had taken with tongs from the altar." There were two altars in the temple—the altar of burnt sacrifice outside the sanctuary and the altar of incense inside the sanctuary. For a variety of reasons, I am convinced that this burning coal is taken from the altar of incense. You see, this all returns to Uzziah and his sin. The place where Uzziah stood in sin is the place where God begins to redeem Isaiah. A seraph flies to that very altar and takes a burning coal with tongs, as if it is so hot and holy even the seraph cannot touch it. He brings it to Isaiah and touches it to his lips, and says, "Behold, this has touched your lips; your guilt is taken away, and your sin atoned for" (v. 7).

There is forgiveness and atonement only in the action of God, and this is a beautiful picture of that salvation. Isaiah stands with nothing to offer the Lord except his sins, which Martin Luther said is true of all of us. As he stands there with his sins, God takes the action, sending the seraph to touch his lips with the coal and say, "Your sin is atoned for."

Normally we think of atonement in relation to the altar of sacrifice in the courtyard of the temple, but in Numbers 16 we read that at the time of the rebellion of Korah, it was the altar of incense that provided atonement. I think we see this also in Isaiah 6. God provides atonement for sin from the place where sin was committed. But the healing, according to Isaiah 6, has not come yet. God has given a wonderful picture of salvation, but the fullness of it still has not come.

Isaiah is commissioned to go and preach, and he is told that he will go the way many preachers feel they have gone—to people who will not listen. God says to him: "Make the heart of this people dull, and their ears heavy, and blind their eyes; lest they see with their eyes, and hear with their ears, and understand with their hearts, and turn and be healed" (v. 10). The time of healing is not yet. The leprosy is not to be taken from the people yet. Why not? Because God has an agent to send, a Servant. Isaiah prophesies of Him in verse 13, where he says the nation will be destroyed and cut down like an oak tree, but the seed of holiness will remain in its stump. God is yet going to do something for His people. He is yet going to send that seed of holiness, the seed in the stump of David, the seed who will be a Redeemer.

The Vision of the Servant

That takes us to Isaiah 52 and 53. There Isaiah has his glorious vision of what this seed, this Servant, will be like. This is a passage of beauty and profundity, but also of great familiarity, such that we may be slightly deaf to its message. Therefore, I would like to walk through it with Uzziah in the backs of our minds. I don't believe that thinking about Uzziah in relation to Isaiah 52–53 exhausts the passage by any means. I am not even sure it is the most important element of the passage. But I think it gives us a different angle on the passage to understand something more of the Servant whom God sends.

The Servant, we know, is our Lord Jesus Christ. Isaiah begins to speak of Him in 52:13: "Behold, my servant shall act wisely; he shall be high and lifted up." This was not true of Uzziah. Only great David's greater Son, our Lord Jesus, is worthy to be compared to the Lord God as the one high and lifted up. Here is a glorious, divine King. He is described in the same language that described the Lord God in His temple in Isaiah 6.

The prophecy continues, "So shall he sprinkle many nations" (v. 15a). This Servant is a Priest-King. One of the actions of a priest in Old Testament Israel was to sprinkle the people with blood in all sorts of circumstances. Moses did that at the founding of the Mosaic covenant at Sinai. There was a sprinkling of blood annually in relation to the Day of Atonement. There was a sprinkling of blood whenever someone claimed to be cleansed from leprosy—there would be a sacrifice, then the priest would take blood and sprinkle it on the leper as a sign of cleansing. Here we are introduced to God's Servant, our Lord Jesus Christ, as a Priest-King. Part of the reason why God said in the Old Testament that His kings could not go into the temple was that only the Messiah would unify kingship and priesthood. Only the Messiah would be a Priest-King. By going into the sanctuary, Uzziah proclaimed to the world, "I am Messiah!" God said: "No, you are not. You are a sinner." Today we live in a world of people who stand up and say, "I am Messiah." Every one of us is tempted to do it. To everyone except our Lord Jesus Christ, God says: "You are not Messiah. You are a sinner. You are a leper."

Further we read, "As many were astonished at you—his appearance was so marred, beyond human resemblance, and his form beyond that of the children of mankind" (v. 14). And then, "He was despised and rejected by men; a man of sorrows, and acquainted with grief; and as one from whom men hide their faces he was despised, and we esteemed him not" (53:3). At least in part, I believe these prophecies are saying that Jesus is our Priest-King *and* Jesus is a leper. Isaiah writes, "His appearance was so marred, beyond human semblance." I am not saying that description is exclusively fulfilled in the idea of leprosy, but I think it suggests the idea of leprosy. It is the same with the words, "He was despised and rejected by men; a man of sorrows, and acquainted with grief." The word translated as "grief" here also can be translated as "sickness." They are related notions. Jesus was acquainted with the sickness of leprosy, and so we hid our faces from Him and despised Him, as we despise all lepers.

Are you beginning to see what it cost Jesus Christ to be the Savior? When we say He is King, that sounds pretty good. Even when we say He is Priest, that is honorable. He is those things. But the depth of our salvation is to be found in the willingness of Jesus to become a leper for sinners. Surely He has borne our sickness.

Seeing the Horror of the Cross

Of course, Jesus was not literally a leper. He was not literally afflicted with the disease of leprosy. But just as Uzziah the good king was afflicted with leprosy to show the people the sinfulness of sin, in some sense, I believe, we have to think of Jesus as a leper to begin to realize the depths of what it meant for Him to take our sin on Himself. We so blithely can say, "He made him to be sin who knew no sin, so that in him we might become the righteousness of God" (2 Cor. 5:21). It seems an easy transaction. How hard could sin-bearing have been for the eternal Son of God? We do not really believe it was an easy thing, but we can unintentionally slip into that attitude. The atonement becomes too familiar. "What a nice thing the cross is," we think. "Jesus did a nice thing that day."

We need to see the horror of the cross. He who from all eternity had been seated on the throne of heaven; of whom the surrounding angels sang, "Holy, holy, holy"; He who was beautiful and majestic in glory, purity, and power—that One became so corrupt that we cannot look at Him. We turn our heads and close our eyes; the deformity is too shocking. The seraphim could not look at Him because of His glory, and they covered their eyes. But throughout His life and especially on the cross, we cannot look at Him because of the horror of the sin that He took upon Himself, not just Uzziah's leprosy, but the leprosy of every one of His people. Think of the weight of sin added to sin added to sin added to sin. How long do we have to say that to begin even to approach the burden that He bore?

Isaiah 53 celebrates the truth that Jesus became our substitute. He took the sinner's place. He entered into the place where Uzziah had been stricken with leprosy. We read in 2 Chronicles 26 that Uzziah was cut off from the house of the Lord for the rest of his life. What does Isaiah 53 tell us? Jesus was cut off from the land of the living (v. 8). He was separated from life. He was separated from His Father. He was separated from His people. He was cut off. He had become the sin-bearer.

In Isaiah 53:4 we read, "Surely he has borne our griefs and carried our sorrows; yet we esteemed him stricken, smitten by God, and afflicted." *Stricken* is that word that is used over and over again in Leviticus to talk about lepers. They are said to be stricken with the disease. *Smitten* is another word that is sometimes used relative to those who suffer from leprosy. Again, I am not saying this exhausts the meaning of these words, but it brings us back to the context of leprosy: Jesus is the One who is afflicted, stricken, and smitten by God. This is a picture of what it takes to save sinners, of what it cost our Jesus to take our place, so that we might be healed.

Isaiah goes on: "He was wounded for our transgressions; he was crushed for our iniquities; upon him was the chastisement that brought us peace, and with his stripes we are healed" (v. 5). Jesus is the atoning sacrifice. He is the only way to forgiveness, and it is in His suffering, His bleeding, His dying, His bearing of the wrath of God on the cross that at last our leprosy is healed. At last our guilt is taken away. What was done for us results in a whole different relationship to God. Now we can call God "Father," because, in a sense, for a time, Jesus lost His Father.

Do you begin to see the love of the Savior in this? Do you see the cost of the cross? Do you see what it takes for sin to be forgiven? Remember that quote from Robert McAfee Brown: "I like sinning and God likes forgiving, and the world is well put together"? What a tragic lie. What a demeaning of the Savior. But we tend to live like that, don't we? I'm a Christian, so I can sneak in a little sin, because it's all been paid for. Sin upon sin upon sin upon sin upon sin, all laid on the Savior on the cross. It is no trivial thing.

When Jesus died, He was buried with the wicked (Isa. 53:9a). I think there may be an allusion to Uzziah even here. We know that Jesus was buried in the tomb of Joseph of Arimathea, but in a sense He was buried with the kings of Israel. When He was buried, the sign over Jesus' tomb read, in a sense, "He is a leper," because He bore our sins and carried our sorrows. It is an amazing picture.

The Conqueror and the Intercessor

At the end of this wonderful chapter, in verse 12a, we return to this theme of Jesus as the Priest-King. Isaiah writes: "Therefore I will divide him a portion with the many, and he shall divide the spoil with the strong." He is our King victorious—victorious over sin, death, and the Devil, risen to reign forever. He did not remain in the grave as a leper, but rose as God's glorious King, the Conqueror, the One who rides forth as King of kings and Lord of lords, conquering and to conquer, in order to gather His people and give gifts to men. This is the picture of the resurrected Christ as King, the Christ who is forever the Priest-King, "because he poured out his soul to death and was numbered with the transgressors; yet he bore the sin of many" (v. 12b), of all His people. If you belong to Jesus

Christ, He bore your sins. He bore them all on the cross. That is a glorious thing, not a trivial thing.

Now He "makes intercession for the transgressors" (v. 12c). He not only died once for all on the cross, to bear all the penalty, but He ever lives to intercede for you and me (Heb. 7:25). Sometimes sin becomes a huge weight on us as Christians. We may know in our minds that Christ has paid the penalty for our sins, but sometimes our sin oppresses us. At such times, Hebrews 7:25 is a wonderful promise. It tells us He ever lives to pray for us. He does not forget us. He has not finished His work and moved on. He is praying for us as His people. We need to be encouraged in the struggle against sin by the fact that He ever lives to intercede for us. He is our Priest-King, who was a leper, but now lives and reigns forever.

The cross stands at the very heart and center of history. It was prepared by God through all those centuries, through all those pictures. God knew how stupid we are and how slow we are to believe. He knew that there would be many who would not believe the report, and so, with picture after picture, He prepared us, so that when Jesus was lifted on the cross we would know what it meant.

Therefore, when Jesus saw the cross approaching, He said in effect: "There I will be glorified, because there I will fulfill history. There I will fulfill the redemptive plan that has been in place from all eternity. There I will pay the penalty for the sin of My people. There I will be glorified because I will accomplish all righteousness and all salvation. There I will atone for sin." Jesus literally said: "And I, when I am lifted up from the earth,"—not in the pride of Uzziah, but in the glory of the Father—"will draw all people to myself" (John 12:32). Do you see Him, both high and lifted up in glory, and high and lifted up as a leper, that lepers might come and find life and hope?

David, that great prophet, wrote:

"I love the Lord, because he has heard
my voice and my pleas for mercy.

Because he inclined his ear to me,
therefore I will call on him as long as I live.
The snares of death
encompassed me;
the pangs of Sheol laid hold on me;
I suffered distress and anguish.
Then I called on the name of the LORD:
'O LORD, I pray, deliver my soul!'
Gracious is the LORD, and righteous;
our God is merciful. . . .
For you have delivered my soul from death,
my eyes from tears,
my feet from stumbling;
I will walk before the LORD
in the land of the living." (Ps. 116:1–9)

Jesus was cut off from the land of the living so that you might walk before the Lord in the land of the living. Praise God for our leprous High Priest.

Notes

1   John Calvin, *Institutes of the Christian Religion*, Library of Christian Classics, vols. XX–XXI, ed. John T. McNeill, trans. Ford Lewis Battles (Louisville: Westminster John Knox, 1960), 1.1.1.

2   John Calvin, *Commentary on the Last Four Books of Moses Arranged in a Harmony* (Grand Rapids: Baker, 1979), 3:346.

8

"YOU SHALL BE HOLY":

THE NECESSITY
OF SANCTIFICATION

- Derek W. H. Thomas -

It is one thing to talk about the holiness of God; it is another thing to desire holiness for ourselves. Yet holiness is an essential aspect of the Christian life. I think of Martin Luther's great stress on a faith that produces works. Then there is John Calvin's teaching in his *Institutes of the Christian Religion* as to the third use of the law of God (*tertius usus legis*) as a guide for sanctification. Likewise, there is the affirmation in the Westminster Confession of Faith that we are justified by faith alone, but the faith that justifies is not alone—it is always accompanied by works (11.2). Yet we live in a man-centered age and worship in man-centered churches. We live for self-fulfillment rather than to please God. We like books on how to be good fathers, how to be successful lovers, or how to improve our diets rather than books that explain to us how we can be holy and Christlike. Sometimes, in Reformed circles, we can be so easily concerned about theological issues that we miss the point. The point of all theology is to drive us to Christlikeness, to holiness of life, and to worship.

Some of us are familiar with the words of Robert Murray McCheyne, that great Scottish minister of the nineteenth century. He lived only until the age of twenty-nine and was in the ministry for only seven years, and at least one of those years he was in Palestine forming what would become a mission to the Jews. But despite his youth, he understood the importance of holiness. "My people's greatest need," he said, speaking as a minister, "is my personal holiness." He understood that holiness is a serious business, because, as the author of Hebrews puts it, without holiness no man shall see the Lord (Heb. 12:14).

As we think about this topic, I'd like us to look at 1 Peter 1. It reads in part:

> Therefore, preparing your minds for action, and being sober-minded, set your hope fully on the grace that will be brought to you at the revelation of Jesus Christ. As obedient children, do not be conformed to the passions of your former ignorance, but as he who called you is holy, you also be holy in all your conduct, since it is written, "You shall be holy, for I am holy." And if you call on him as Father who judges impartially according to each one's deeds, conduct yourselves with fear throughout the time of your exile, knowing that you were ransomed from the futile ways inherited from your forefathers, not with perishable things such as silver or gold, but with the precious blood of Christ, like that of a lamb without blemish or spot. He was foreknown before the foundation of the world but was made manifest in the last times for the sake of you who through him are believers in God, who raised him from the dead and gave him glory, so that your faith and hope are in God. Having purified your souls by your obedience to the truth for a sincere brotherly love, love one

another earnestly from a pure heart, since you have been born again, not of perishable seed but of imperishable, through the living and abiding word of God; for "All flesh is like grass and all its glory like the flower of grass. The grass withers, and the flower falls, but the word of the Lord remains forever." And this word is the good news that was preached to you. (vv. 13–25)

As you can see, this passage begins with the word *therefore*. As preachers are wont to say, when you see the word *therefore*, you must ask the question, "What is the *therefore* there for?" In this case, it is there because it is introducing us to gospel grammar; that is, Peter wants to address the issue of holiness and sanctification in relationship to the gospel. He wants to say some very specific things in the course of this letter, but he is basing his moral, ethical imperatives on gospel indicatives, which underline our prior right standing (justification) with God. If we confuse the order of these two—that is, if we confuse sanctification and justification—we confuse the gospel.

From Indicatives to Imperatives

In the opening section of this epistle, Peter introduces us to certain indicatives, certain things that are true about us as the people of God, as those who have come to faith in Jesus Christ. In the opening two verses of chapter 1, he addresses "elect exiles of the dispersion of Pontus, Galatia, Cappadocia, Asia, and Bithynia" (v. 1b), what we think of today as Asia Minor or Turkey. He declares that they are elect "according to the foreknowledge of God the Father, in the sanctification of the Spirit, for obedience to Jesus Christ" (v. 2a). So at the very outset, he introduces the goal of this epistle. He wants us to see that in the plan and purpose of God, the whole scheme of the plan of redemption, from the secret counsels of God in eternity until the very last day, is the sanctification of believers in the Spirit for obedience to Jesus Christ. In short, we are saved to be holy. We are justified by faith in order that we might reflect something of the holiness of God.

Notice how trinitarian Peter is. He mentions "the foreknowledge of God the Father," "the sanctification of the Spirit," and "obedience to Jesus Christ." It is as though the Father is looking down the corridors of history and has already set His love on this one and that one, and He turns to the Holy Spirit and says, "In my love, I want this one to become Mine." The Spirit taps on that person's shoulder and says, "The Father wants you." The Spirit takes that person to Jesus Christ and says, "This one wants You to be his Prophet, his Priest, and his King." Jesus says to the person, "Come and meet My Father, because it was His plan all along."

Furthermore, Peter says we have been called to a living hope, an indescribable inheritance, and an inexpressible joy in Christ (vv. 3–7). This is what we have as those who have been drawn by the Spirit into union and communion with Jesus Christ. On the basis of this, of what we now are in Jesus Christ, we are to be holy. We are to be sanctified. We are to be Christlike.

Notice, then, the relationship between the indicative and the imperative. Peter is not calling on us to be holy in order that we might be saved, but because we are already in union with Christ. Since we are already the redeemed of the Lord, now, as a consequence, we are to be holy. Getting that order right is perhaps the most important thing we can ever learn about holiness. This, then, is the background for the "therefore" in verse 13.

Notice, too, how Peter begins, for it is counterintuitive. He writes, "Therefore, preparing your minds for action . . ." The King James Version puts it this way: "Gird up the loins of your mind . . ." Back in 1972 or '73, I picked up a little booklet written by John Stott, and the opening sentence of that booklet read something like this: "The major secret of holy living lies in the mind." Holy living begins with how we think. It begins with an epistemological repentance. It begins with changing our minds about certain things and having our minds addressed by the Word of God. "Preparing your minds for action" means beginning to think in Christian ways, in biblical ways.

Not long after that, I was introduced to John Owen. As a young Christian, I stayed for about a year or so in the manse of Geoffrey Thomas, the Reformed Baptist preacher at Alfred Place in Aberystwyth, where he has now been for almost forty-five years. He decided that one of the things I needed most was to get up early, and I think it was around 5 o'clock in the morning. The two of us would drink very strong coffee—black, no sugar—and we would read volume 7 of John Owen's *Works*, the section on spiritual-mindedness. Owen can be prolix; he subscribed to the philosophy, "Why say something in a hundred words when you can take a thousand?" I remember writing little notes in the margins of my volume 7 of Owen at 5 or 5:30 in the morning. Those notes are incomprehensible now. But I do remember one statement that Owen made. It was in the form of a question: "What do you think about when you are not thinking about anything in particular?" In other words, what is the default setting of your mind? What do you revert to when you are not being forced to go in a certain direction? That, Owen says, is the indicator of your spiritual-mindedness. It is the indicator of your holiness.

Peter says, "Gird up the loins of your mind." In other words, we need to begin to think in biblical categories and biblical terms. He then proceeds to set before us a number of motivations for holiness, and I want to explore three of these in the remainder of this chapter.

Motivation #1: God's Holiness

The first motivation is the holiness of God Himself. In verse 16, Peter cites a text from the book of Leviticus, the so-called "holiness code": "You shall be holy, for I am holy" (see Lev. 11:44–45; 19:2; 20:26; 21:8). This gives us a motivation and perhaps also a standard for holiness. Because God—Father, Son, and Holy Spirit—is holy, He wants His people to be holy. We have been drawn into a relationship with this God. He is our Creator, who made us in order that we might reflect His holiness. He then re-created us, quickening us through the instrumentality of the Word, and through the gospel He has brought us to the feet of Jesus Christ, whom we have embraced by faith as Prophet, Priest, and King. He did all of this so that we might be holy, that we might be sanctified, that we might be set apart, that we might reflect something of His moral purity and integrity. How could the Creator and Re-Creator God not want us to be a holy people, set apart for Him, living out-and-out for Him, putting Him first in every aspect of our lives?

In the opening chapters of 1 Samuel, we encounter Hannah, Samuel's mother, who was motivated to be holy by a consideration of the holiness of God. We are introduced to this little family, which consisted of Elkanah and his wife Hannah, whom Elkanah loved. But there was another woman, Peninnah, Elkanah's second wife. That should set off alarm bells in our minds—there were significant problems here. As we read the chapter, we find that Hannah had no children and seemingly could not conceive. But Peninnah was having children as often as fruit drops off the trees in the fall, and she was proud of it. On visits to the sanctuary at Shiloh, Peninnah, snooty little thing that she appears to have been, rubbed it in. You can imagine Peninnah's children asking, "Why doesn't Aunty Hannah have children?" Peninnah might have replied: "Well, I don't know. Why don't you go ask her?"

One year, when the family reached Shiloh, Hannah was weeping and would not eat. She was in spiritual torment and trial. Elkanah, who must not have read "How to Be a Good Husband," said to her: "Hannah, why do you weep? And why do you not eat? And why is your heart sad? Am I not more to you than ten sons?" (v. 8). What an oaf. Later, Hannah went to the temple, where Eli the priest was sitting. She was praying and her lips were moving, but she was making no sound. Eli, who had been reading the same journal about male sensitivity as Elkanah, said, "How long will you go on being drunk?" (v. 14). But in her prayer, Hannah did an incredible thing. It moved me beyond description as I reflected on this passage. She prayed, "Lord give me a son, and I will give him back to You" (see v. 11). That was her prayer in the midst of her trial and her pain.

In 1 Peter, the apostle is writing to a church that is facing trial. He is writing probably in the mid- to late '60s, about the time of the onset of Roman persecution against the church. He is trying to prepare his readers for the day of trial, and he wants them to see that in that day they must be holy because God is holy. If we turn back to 1 Samuel and look at chapter 2, we see that when God answered Hannah's prayer for a son, she sang a glorious song. Mary cites it almost verbatim in the Magnificat (Luke 1:46–55). Hannah said, "There is none holy like the LORD; there is none besides you" (v. 2a). What enabled Hannah to reflect that consecrated spirit, to pray that selfless prayer, "Lord, give me a son, and I will give him back to you"? Later, when Samuel was three or four, when he had been weaned, she took him to Shiloh and left him there. Can you even imagine what that was like? Can you imagine the selflessness of it? What enabled her to deny herself in this way? The holiness of God shaped and molded the pattern of her holy living. Don't you think that is what Peter is talking about when he is preparing the dispersed Christians to face the onset of trial and difficulty?

Maybe you are facing unimaginable trials and difficulties, so maybe you are thinking: "How in the world can I be holy when I've got this trial? If the Lord would take this trial away, then I might be holy." But God is saying: "This is why the trial is there. It is to *make* you holy. It is to bring you to an end of yourself."

The holiness of God is attractive; that is why Psalm 29:2 speaks of "the splendor of holiness." Holiness can be intimidating, but there is a beauty to holiness too. We see that in Isaiah 6, where the prophet, in his vision of God in His heavenly temple, feels repulsion, but also an attraction.

Don't you think that Peter is saying here, speaking in the context of oncoming trials, that in the midst of your pain, in the midst of your difficulty, in the midst of the horrendousness of it all, only God can fully satisfy, because it was by Him you were made and it was by Him you were re-made in Jesus Christ? Therefore, be holy because God is holy.

Now, I think it is all too easy for us to talk about the holiness of God, to have R. C. Sproul's magnificent exposition of that holiness on our bookshelves, to sort of carry the topic of holiness around as an emblem of our Reformed status. But God is interested in the state of our hearts and souls. He is saying to you and me, "I want you to be holy." Is that your passionate concern? Is that your overwhelming interest? Is that the thing you long for, pray for, and seek after more than anything else in all the world? Do you say: "I want to be a holy person; I want to be known as somebody who is Christlike, self-denying as Jesus was"?

Motivation #2: The Gospel

There is a second motivation here—the gospel. Peter expounds this motivation in verses 17–21.

Peter first evokes reverent obedience: "And if you call on him as Father who judges impartially according to each one's deeds, conduct yourselves with fear throughout the time of your exile, knowing that you were ransomed from the futile ways inherited from your forefathers, not with perishable things such as silver or gold, but with the precious blood of Christ, like that of a lamb without blemish or spot" (vv. 17–19).

Peter seems to be saying at least two things here. First, he is telling us that the motivation of the gospel is depicted for us by the language and significance of redemption. We were purchased by the blood of Jesus Christ, which is that of a lamb without spot or blemish. You and I as believers in Jesus Christ have been bought. We are not our own.

Second, Peter is meditating, I think, as he so often did, on an incident at Caesarea Philippi, recorded for us in Matthew 16:13–23. Jesus asked the disciples, "Who do people say that the Son of Man is?" They replied that some said He was John the Baptist, some said Elijah, some said Jeremiah, and others said He was some other prophet. Then He asked, "But who do you say that I am?" Peter, this Peter, said, "You are the Christ, the Son of the

Living God." Jesus told him, "You are Peter, and on this rock I will build my church, and the gates of hell shall not prevail against it." Jesus went on, you remember, to say that He must go to Jerusalem and there be handed over to the scribes and Pharisees to be crucified, and on the third day rise again. In response to the thought that his Savior must shed His blood and die in Jerusalem, Peter uttered those two words that can never go together in the same sentence: "Lord, never!" for which he received Jesus' rebuke. I think Peter must have reflected often on that incident.

It is sometimes said that all of Western civilization is just a series of footnotes on Plato and Aristotle. In a sense, all of the New Testament is just a series of footnotes on those words of Jesus at Caesarea Philippi. I think what dawned on Peter that day—and I think it dawned on him for many a day thereafter—was that the blood of Jesus had actually purchased him, so that he was no longer his own, and that the blood of Jesus had redeemed him from his futile, empty way of life, from the vanity of this world.

But not only did Peter see the gospel logic that we are bought, I think he saw that when we purchase something, we have the right to use it in a way that pleases us. It is called the right to private ownership. It is a precious, precious truth. I think Peter is reflecting here on the fact that our holiness is motivated by the truth that we are not our own. We belong to another, to our Savior, Jesus Christ. He purchased us by shedding His blood for us. He paid the ransom price to set us free. Therefore, He may do with us whatsoever He wills.

Peter goes on in verses 20–21 to reflect on the revelation of the gospel: "He [Jesus] was foreknown before the foundation of the world, but was made manifest in the last times for the sake of you, who through him are believers in God, who raised him from the dead and gave him glory, so that your faith and hope are in God." Peter is saying, "This is what the gospel is all about." If we are to be holy, that holiness of ours is fundamentally related to all that God has done in the purposes of redemption, in sending the Lord Jesus Christ into the world to become incarnate, to die on the cross, and to rise again for our justification.

Abraham Kuyper writes, "What the redeemed soul needs is human holiness."[1] He was speaking not of God's holiness or angelic holiness, but human holiness, holiness in the humanity of Jesus Christ. As the author of Hebrews says, "He who sanctifies and those who are sanctified all have one source" (2:11). We share in the holiness of Jesus Christ. We are in progressive sanctification to reflect that righteousness of Christ that God has reckoned and imputed to us by faith in Him.

God does this, first of all, by bringing us into gospel union with Jesus Christ. In Paul's language, we are "in Christ," having "believed *into* Jesus Christ" (see Gal. 2:16).

Peter puts it this way: We are "living stones" (1 Peter 2:5). Isn't it interesting that the one Jesus addressed as "the rock" was the one who said we are living stones in a temple in which Jesus Christ is the chief cornerstone? We are to be holy because we have been brought by faith into a living and vital relationship with Jesus Christ.

Motivation #3: The Relationship

Notice that there is a third motivation. Peter tells us that we are children, and it is a great privilege to call on the Father (1:17). We have been brought into a relationship in which we can call God, this holy God, our "Abba, Father" (Rom. 8:15; Gal. 4:6). We are the children of God. We have been brought into His family. That is why, I think, Peter goes on in this passage to speak about loving one another (v. 22); it is because we have to be conscious that as Christians we have been brought into a family.

I wasn't raised in a Christian home. I never went to church as a boy. I never read the Bible and didn't possess a copy of it. I couldn't have told you what was in the Bible. I remember as a young Christian, having been suddenly converted in 1971 through reading a book, my first occasion of walking into a Reformed Baptist church and seeing men and women carrying Bibles and talking about Jesus. I had been raised in a somewhat dysfunctional family, and I remember thinking then a thought that has never gone away: "This is my family. These are my mothers and fathers and brothers and sisters and wives and husbands. These are my people." Don't you sense that when you go to church? You realize that the people there are your people. You share the same interests, the same goals. You read the same books. You talk about the same things. You have the same interests.

Peter is addressing holiness within the context of family life. Remember that you are in the family of God now.

When I was twelve or thirteen, my older brother was seventeen. You know how it is when you are in your teens—four years can be like fifty years. When you're thirteen and your older brother is seventeen, he might as well be sixty-three. I did something in high school and got in trouble with the headmaster. As punishment, I was caned by the headmaster, which was legal at the time. But that was nothing. At lunchtime, my seventeen-year-old brother caught me in the corridor, pulled me aside, and took me out behind the proverbial woodshed—in this case, it was a shed that held sports equipment. Behind the shed, he uttered these words, which have never gone away from me: "You've let the family down." It was like some Sicilian Mafia boss speaking to me.

This is Peter's motivation: We are to love one another from a pure heart, with sincerity and affection, because we are members of the family of God. When you sin, when you fall short of God's glory, you let the family down. You let your Father down. Your conduct is a test of your love for our heavenly Father. His holiness is to be our overwhelming desire, our aspiration.

Embrace the Trials

Now, there are other motivations here, not the least of which is the idea of the judgment of God (v. 17). What ever happened to the judgment of God in evangelical churches? What ever happened to the notion that for the redeemed of the Lord, there will be a judgment according to works, that we must give an account of all the deeds that we've done in the body, and that there are rewards in the new heaven and new earth. Somehow, in the past twenty or thirty years, the idea of egalitarianism has crept into the evangelical church's concept of the new heaven and the new earth. But that is not what the New Testament seems to be teaching here. One of the motivations for holiness is that we must give an account, that a day of reckoning is coming.

Peter's concern for holiness is in the midst of fiery trials. Is that where you are? Are you passing through a particular trial, a horrendous difficulty in your marriage, in your work, with your children, with yourself? Peter would say: "I want you to see that trial as God's gift to you." Whatever your trial is, embrace it. Don't waste your cancer, as John Piper says.[2] Don't waste your trial, but see it, in the purposes of our sovereign God, as the very means to conform you to the image of His Son, that you might be able to say with Job, "When he hath tried me, I shall come forth as gold" (Job 23:10, KJV).

Charles Wesley wrote these stirring hymn lyrics:

Finish, then, thy new creation;
Pure and spotless let us be;
Let us see thy great salvation
Perfectly restored in thee;
Changed from glory into glory,
Till in heaven we take our place,
Till we cast our crowns before thee,
Lost in wonder, love, and praise.[3]

God says, "You shall be holy, for I am holy." Therefore, so do.

Notes

1 Abraham Kuyper, *The Work of the Holy Spirit* (1900; repr., Grand Rapids: Eerdmans, 1975), 461.

2 John Piper, "Don't Waste Your Cancer," Desiring God Resource Library, Feb. 15, 2006, http://www.desiringgod.org/ResourceLibrary/TasteAndSee/ByDate/2006/1776_Dont_Waste_Your_Cancer/

3 From the hymn "Love Divine, All Loves Excelling" by Charles Wesley, 1747.

9

"TRAIN UP A CHILD":

WALKING TOGETHER WITH THE HOLY GOD

- R. C. Sproul Jr. -

THINK WITH ME FOR A FEW MOMENTS ABOUT Exodus 3, beginning in verse 1:

> Now, Moses was keeping the flock of his father-in-law, Jethro, the priest of Midian, and he led his flock to the west side of the wilderness and came to Horeb, the mountain of God. The angel of the LORD appeared to him in a flame of fire out of the midst of a bush. He looked, and behold, the bush was burning, yet it was not consumed. And Moses said, "I will turn aside to see this great sight, why the bush is not burned." When the LORD saw that he turned aside to see, God called to him out of the bush, "Moses, Moses!" And he said, "Here I am." Then he said, "Do not come near; take

your sandals off your feet, for the place on which you are standing is holy ground." And he said, "I am the God of your father, the God of Abraham, the God of Isaac, and the God of Jacob." And Moses hid his face, for he was afraid to look at God. . . . Then Moses said to God, "If I come to the people of Israel and say to them, 'The God of your fathers has sent me to you,' and they ask me, 'What is his name?' what shall I say to them?" God said to Moses, "I AM WHO I AM." And he said, "Say this to the people of Israel, 'I AM has sent me to you.'" God also said to Moses, "Say to the people of Israel, 'The LORD, the God of our fathers, the God of Abraham, the God of Isaac, and the God of Jacob, has sent me to you.' This is my name forever, and thus I am to be remembered throughout all generations." (vv. 1–6, 13–15)

I have a compulsion. I have a burning, insatiable desire to which I am so given that I don't even bother to fight it. I confess that I am a compulsive reader. I can't stop reading. I read in the morning. I read during the day. I read at night. I wake up in the middle of the night so I can read.

Of course, all that reading doesn't necessarily mean that I have a whole lot of good stuff in my brain. I will read anything to satisfy my compulsion. When I sit down to eat my breakfast—which I also do quite a lot—I read cereal boxes. Likewise, when I'm on an airplane, I read everything they give me. Thanks to that reading, I know what the law says about how the airlines have to compensate you if they lose your luggage.

I have read some strange things on airplanes. For instance, I have read *Skymall*, the catalog of trinkets that every airline seems to offer. Have you seen this? Would you ever in your life think to yourself, "I need a crossword puzzle as big as a wall"? Are you so compassionate that you think, "It saddens me that my dog has to bend all the way down to the floor to eat his food, so I'll buy a special table for his food so he can eat more comfortably"? These are things you can get in a *Skymall* catalog.

Here's something else you can get: If you're a businessman with no time, there is a service that provides someone to read business books for you and write summaries. If you don't know *Who Moved My Cheese?* they'll tell you. If you don't have quite enough time to move from *Good to Great*, they'll help you get slightly better. This service provides *Cliffs Notes* for busy executives, people who want the bottom line.

A Summary of the Bible

Maybe there is a market for this kind of service in the Christian world. I can imagine a Christian saying: "I don't have time for all this stuff. There are laws in the Bible about what to do in this situation and that situation. There are measurements for the tabernacle and all the furniture therein. There are four Gospels and two letters to the church at Corinth. I can't read all this. It's a thick book and I'm too busy. What's the bottom line? What do I really need to know? If God were to say to me, 'Hey, do this,' what would He tell me?" So what would I put in a summary of the Bible for the busy Christian?

You could argue that it's the so-called "Dominion Mandate," the first command God gave to Adam: "Be fruitful and multiply and fill the earth and subdue it and have dominion over the fish of the sea and over the birds of the heavens and over every living thing that moves on the earth" (Gen. 1:28). God doesn't change, and neither has this command.

You could make the case that it's the great commandment. Jesus said, "You shall love the Lord your God with all your heart and with all your soul and with all you mind and with all your strength" (Mark 12:30). That sounds like a good bottom line.

Solomon, the wisest man ever to walk on the planet (at least in the Old Testament), gave us a clue. He said: "The end of the matter; all has been heard. Fear God and keep his commandments, for this is the whole duty of man" (Eccl. 12:13). Doesn't that sound like an executive summary?

Maybe we find the best summary in the words of the prophet Micah: "He has told you, O man, what is good; and what does the LORD require of you but to do justice, and to love kindness, and to walk humbly with your God?" (Micah 6:8).

But, of course, we're New Testament Christians. There is more there, too, isn't there? We could turn to Matthew's Gospel, where Jesus says, "Seek first the kingdom of God and his righteousness, and all these things will be added unto you" (6:33). The bottom line is this: seek the kingdom of God. But there's also the Great Commission, Jesus' last message on earth: "Go therefore and make disciples of all nations, baptizing them in the name of the Father and of the Son and of the Holy Spirit, teaching them to observe all that I have commanded you" (Matt. 28:19–20a). And there's also Jesus' final admonition to Peter: "Feed my sheep" (John 21:16).

Well, our list of summaries has gotten rather lengthy. It turns out that there is not just one executive summary to the Bible, but several. What do we do about that? How can we summarize all of these summaries? Well, it takes a Presbyterian. When my spiritual ancestors looked at this problem, all of these bottom lines, all of these executive summaries, they said: "Let's narrow it down. What is it we're supposed to do? What is the chief end of man?" They answered this way: "Man's chief end is to glorify God and to enjoy him forever."[1]

Bringing Glory to God

We Reformed folk have a pretty good idea about what it means to glorify God, or at least we think we do. For us, glorifying God means doing great things for His kingdom. We glorify God when we suffer great hardships for His kingdom. We glorify God when we keep a stiff upper lip for His kingdom. Indeed, our visions about what it means to glorify God are wrapped up in our heroes of the faith and our ancestors who went before us. We think of the martyrdoms of Hugh Latimer and Nicholas Ridley. We think of the bold defiance of that great Scottish woman Jenny Geddes, who, when an Anglican clergyman showed up to impose the Book of

Common Prayer, threw her stool at him, and died for it. There is a lot of dying in our vision of what it means to glorify God.

These men and women did glorify God, both in their lives and in their deaths. But not one of them glorified God in their lives or their deaths in the same way or in the same measure that they glorified God after their deaths. It was after they died that they began to glorify God fully. Only then did they truly and fully behold His glory. After we die, we no longer see "through a glass darkly" (1 Cor. 13:12); then we see God as He is. When that happens, we suddenly understand that glorifying God and enjoying God are one and the same. This is why Dr. John Piper never spoke with greater wisdom than when he penned these words: "God is most glorified in us when we are most satisfied in him."[2] And we are most satisfied in Him when we have gone on to our reward, when we behold His glory, when we revel in His holiness, when we become what we were made to be, when we go back to the garden.

You are familiar with Genesis 1 and 2. You are familiar with the account of the fall of Adam and Eve, and you are familiar with what happened before that, with the description of God's grace in their lives even before they fell into sin. God was good to them; He put them in a paradise where the lion lay down with the lamb. There were no animals to fear. There were no thorns or thistles in their labors. There was a man and a woman, and they were without sin and they loved each other. There was no sickness, no death. It was paradise. But where was the real glory there? What we lost in the fall wasn't merely peaceful relations with the animals, the absence of thorns and thistles, and perfect health. The pinnacle of Eden, the absence of which forms the valley of the curse, was that in the garden human beings walked with God.

In chapter 1, my father gives an extraordinary exposition of the character of God, about who God is, about the holiness of God, about His uniqueness, and His aseity, His self-existence. As my father points out, that self-existence is wrapped up in the sacred name of God: "I AM WHO I AM" (Ex. 3:14). We must not lose sight of that name, but I want you to see that there are two names for God in the portion of Exodus 3 that I cited above—two sacred, holy, names. God says: "Say this to the people of Israel, 'The LORD, the God of your fathers, the God of Abraham, the God of Isaac, and the God of Jacob, has sent me to you.' This is my name forever, and thus I am to be remembered throughout all generations" (Ex. 3:15).

My father speaks of the famine in our land, about our failure to understand the transcendent holiness of God, and he is absolutely right. The scariest thing of all is that we are starving ourselves. We teach clergy to conceal the holiness of God, to communicate a God who is imminent, a God who is near, so that people can feel that closeness. We've made God small so that we can reach Him. But our text tells us that this great and mighty God has condescended to be with us. The two names communicate that He is both transcendent and that He is in a relationship with us.

Worshiping God as a Family

This is why our family does not practice family devotions. I stubbornly refuse to practice family devotions, and if you are doing it, I encourage you to stop. You see, the term "family devotions" suggests that we are fulfilling some sort of obligation or duty. It is as if we recognize that God has been very good to us, so we ought to do something to demonstrate our commitment to God and our passion for Him. If that is our thinking, we are behaving just like a Muslim who kneels and prays toward Mecca five times a day out of duty. God forbid!

Instead, our family gathers together to worship God. We draw near to Him. We walk with Him. We delight in Him. We rejoice in Him. The transcendent God invites us to come with our families and walk with Him. The great I AM invites us to be with Him, and He promises that He will be God to us and to our children.

The last thing we want to do is practice family worship for practical reasons. But there are many practical reasons for doing so. One of the blessings of practicing family worship is that it can help quiet down frantic souls in the evening. God has blessed my wife and me with eight children so far. We like calm in the evening, and having a routine and sitting down to worship God as a family can quiet frantic souls. Family worship can be a training ground for children to learn to sit still, be quiet, and participate in corporate worship. Proverbs 22:6 promises, "Train up a child in the way he should go; even when he is old he will not depart from it." But not only do our children learn to worship from us, we learn to worship from them. The Scriptures say, "From the lips of children and infants you have ordained praise" (Ps. 8:2a). Our children help us learn how to worship now as they learn to worship someday.

One of the blessings of family worship is that it is an opportunity to teach our children the content of the Scriptures, the content of our faith. Another blessing is that it is time together as a family. It reminds us of what we are as a family, of our family identity. Yet another blessing of family worship is that it reminds us, and our children, of our chief end. It reminds us that the worship of God is not relegated to Sunday, and maybe Wednesday if we're not busy, but that it infuses and penetrates all of our lives. We understand that when God said we are to give Him one day in seven, He was not saying we could do whatever we want on the other six days. We give Him one day in order to communicate that we recognize every day to be His day. When we gather for family worship, we have much the same blessing.

So the blessings of family worship are many. But if we practice family worship because of these real blessings, we worship ourselves rather than God. Marva Dawn rightly describes worship as "a royal waste of time."[3] What does she mean? She is pointing out that other things we do end up serving other goals. We do this to do that; we do that to do another thing. But with worship, there is nothing more; just as our existence always goes back to God's self-existence, so our end, our purpose, always stops at worship. We don't do worship for the sake of something else. We do everything else for the sake of worship, so we need to stop thinking of it in utilitarian terms. This is what we were made for and how we will spend eternity. Indeed, we do this, to paraphrase C. S. Lewis, "to bring down Deep Heaven on our heads."[4]

Simple Steps for Family Worship

So how do we do this? I'm about to take you through how the Sproul family does family worship. But before I do that, for my own safety and security, I want you to understand why I am doing this. I am not doing this to impose a Sproul Jr. liturgy on you. This is one example. You don't have to follow it, but you can't put this book down and say, "Well, that was great, but I have no idea what to do" (or, "That was horrible, but I have no idea what to do").

Right now in our lives, we practice family worship right after supper. We used to have family worship right before the kids went to bed. Either one is fine for us, but there is a practical reason for doing it in that time frame. Every day, no matter what, we eat supper and we go to bed, so we have a pair of alarm clocks that tell us we cannot escape our call to do this. We think, "Oh, we just finished eating, it's time," or, "We're about to go to bed, it's time."

After supper, I'll ask one of the children, "Please gather the things for worship." We have a place where we keep the worship materials, and one of the children will go and get the stack of books and things, and place it on the table in front of me.

By the way, if we're not at home, we modify things a little bit. We have worship in the car sometimes. If we're at a friend's house or even a stranger's house, we don't impose on him or her and say, "Well, thank you for supper, it's now time for the Sproul family to have worship." If we have a guest at our house, we try to make an assessment of his or her spiritual maturity and then make a decision. We might ask ourselves, "Will this make our guest angry, or will he like this?" If it likely will make him mad, we probably won't do it.

When we are at home, we start with our catechism work. *Catechism* is a word that is unfamiliar to many today. A catechism is simply a tool for teaching basic biblical content to those who are young or new to the faith. A catechism typically consists of questions and answers. The parent asks the child a question, and the child gives the answer.

We use two different catechisms. We have a children's catechism that consists of fifty questions. Each of the questions is five or six words and each of the answers is about three words. I ask my son Reilly, who is three years old, "Reilly, who made you?" Reilly says, "God." I say, "What else did God make?" He says, "Everything." As you can see, the questions and answers are very short. We teach these to the very small children, and when they learn these things, we celebrate. We don't bribe. We don't buy them off. But we do celebrate. When one learns the entire children's catechism, the whole family goes out for ice cream, because Daddy likes ice cream.

When the children get bigger, we move to the Westminster Shorter Catechism, which has slightly longer questions and answers. There are 107 of these. When the children master them all, I take them skiing, because Daddy likes skiing.

We have a "sophisticated" system by which we do the memory work. It goes like this. I say to the children: "Daddy says, 'What is man's chief end?' You say, 'Man's chief end . . .'"

They say, "Man's chief end . . ."

I say, ". . . is to glorify God . . ."

They say, ". . . is to glorify God . . ."

Finally, I say, ". . . and enjoy him forever."

They say, ". . . and enjoy him forever."

We do that, and after a couple of days they get it. As I said, it's a terribly complicated system.

Scripture and Prayer

Then we move on to Bible memory. We have a "complicated" system for that, too. Right now our family is working through the Psalms, so every day we recite one of the psalms we have learned and we work on a new psalm. Don't be overly impressed; we are only up to twelve. I don't know what we're going to do when they get really long. When we get to Psalm 119, then you can be impressed. But again, we use the same system. I say a verse or part of a verse, and the kids repeat it. My older kids make fun of me because I have my Bible open as I'm helping them learn these things, but they know many of the psalms by heart.

Then we move to Scripture reading. We have done our Scripture readings in different ways. Sometimes we read a book of the Bible. Sometimes, when we have a new child who is very small, we use one of the children's Bible storybooks. I want to give them a very basic understanding of the flow of Scripture. Right now we're going through one of those Bible storybooks where Jesus has eyes that look like Ping-Pong balls.

I read the story, then I give my sermon, and my sermons are typically twenty to thirty seconds long. I give the children some sort of lesson from the text. I want to bring the text to bear on their lives and mine.

This gives me an opportunity to practice the first corollary to the "R. C. Sproul Jr. principle of hermeneutics." Hermeneutics is the study of interpretation, and the R. C. Sproul Jr. principle of hermeneutics states that whenever you are reading your Bible and you see someone doing something really stupid, you must not say to yourself, "How can he be so stupid?" but "How am I more stupid?" The first corollary to this principle is that whenever you are reading a story in the Bible and you wonder who you are in the story, you are the sinner. If you are reading a story and there is more than one sinner, as in the parable of the prodigal son, you're both. So we read our Bible text and I ask: "Children, how are we like this person? And how are we like that person? And how am I like this person or that person?" That's the sermon.

After the sermon, I take prayer requests. I ask, "Children, what would you like Daddy to pray for tonight?" Now, I encourage my children to pray. They pray before they go to bed. They pray at times during home-school. They pray on many occasions. But when we gather together for family worship, they don't pray. Why not? From the beginning, I have done the praying at family worship because I want to communicate to them—and, more importantly, to myself—the importance of the father's priestly role in the home. I am saying to them and to myself, "I am responsible, as the head of this home, to take you before the throne of God, to beseech the God of heaven and earth for your wellbeing."

In fact, when the children were younger, we even had a posture to help communicate this—again, more to me than to them. I would ask the little ones to come sit on my lap. I would take one on each leg, put my arms around the children, put my hands over their heads, and pray for them. I would ask God to bless them specifically. My son Campbell would ask every night, "Please ask God that we would grow in grace, in the fruit of the spirit, and in wisdom." God has blessed him with wisdom.

Concluding with Song

Then we move into singing. Again, the children are invited to participate by choosing what we are going to sing. We sing the service music from our church's liturgy. We sing the Gloria Patri. We sing the Doxology. We sing the Apostles' Creed or the Nicene Creed. We sing the Song of Simeon, which is how our church closes its service.

Let me tell you about something that is even more practical. When visitors to Saint Peter Church try to find the nursery, we tell them we do have a nursery, but we hope they won't mind serving in the nursery on that particular day. We assure them that if they'll look after their children, we'll be fine. You see, we worship together—parents and children. Visitors are afraid and puzzled about this. They think, "What kind of weird thing is this?" Then, when we in the congregation stand to confess our faith together and little two- and three-year-olds ardently recite the Apostles' Creed, suddenly our visitors see the beauty of it.

We let our children pick the songs they want to sing. We do have one rule—only one child's song a night. Reilly always wants to sing "Hallelu." I'll ask, "What do you want to sing tonight, Reilly?" and he'll say, "Hallelu." It's a very simple song: "Hallelu, hallelu, hallelu, hallelujah, praise ye the Lord!" We divide the family in half, and half of them are the "hallelus" and half of them are the "praise ye the Lords," then after the first verse we switch and do it faster. But we sing only one of these a night.

That's it. It's not complicated. It's not time-consuming. It's not a duty. It's a joy, a delight.

At this point, you fathers might be thinking, "OK, R. C., I see this. I see that I ought to do this. I see how to do it. But what do I do about the fact that I haven't been doing this?" Here's what you do: Gather your family together, sit them down, and then tell them that you are sorry for failing them in this way. Show them what repentance looks like. Then tell them that Jesus Christ came to suffer the wrath of God the Father for failures such as this. Give thanks for that provision. Pray in thanksgiving for that forgiveness. Then sing in thanksgiving for that forgiveness. That is day one. If you have done this in the past and have fallen out of the habit, simply follow the same instructions.

But if you are too busy, here is what I want you to do: stop being too busy! What could possibly be more important? The God of heaven and earth, the self-existent, transcendent, holy God, is inviting you to walk with Him in the cool of the evening. Will you say to Him, "Thanks for the invitation, Lord, but I've got my bowling league tonight." Would you tell Him, "I'd love to meet with You tonight, but I have a meeting with someone important." No one is too busy to draw near to the living God. No one is too busy to give up the less important, the less rewarding, and the less joyful for the source of all joy.

Lewis said:

If we consider the unblushing promises of reward and the staggering nature of the rewards promised in the gospels, it would seem that our Lord finds our desires not too strong, but too weak. We are half-hearted creatures, fooling around with drink and sex and ambition when infinite joy is offered us, like an ignorant child who wants to go on making mud pies in the slum because he cannot imagine what is meant by an offer of a holiday at sea. We are far too easily pleased.[5]

The glory of the gospel is that the high, transcendent, exultant God, because of the work of Christ, has drawn near to us and to our children, and will continue to do so. Therefore, don't do this in order to be holy. Do it to be happy. In the end, it's the same thing. Our austere pursuit of personal holiness doesn't impress God one bit. But God delights when we delight in Him. Bring the children; suffer the children to come unto Him (Matt. 19:14). Do this so that you might glorify and enjoy Him now, for this is what we will be doing forever.

Notes

1 Westminster Shorter Catechism, Q&A 1.

2 John Piper, *Desiring God: Meditations of a Christian Hedonist* (Sisters, Ore.: Multnomah, 1996), 50.

3 Marva J. Dawn, *A Royal "Waste" of Time: The Splendor of Worshiping God and Being Church for the World* (Grand Rapids: Eerdmans, 1999).

4 C. S. Lewis, *That Hideous Strength* (New York: MacMillan, 1965), 294.

5 C. S. Lewis, *The Weight of Glory and Other Addresses* (New York: HarperCollins, 2001), 16.

10

"A CONSUMING FIRE":

HOLINESS, WRATH, AND JUSTICE

- R. C. Sproul -

WE LIVE IN A CULTURE WHERE THE VAST MAJORITY of the people occasionally gives lip service to the existence of God but almost never regards Him as holy. If some do acknowledge that He is holy, very few add to that holiness any idea of divine justice. And if we are able to find a handful of people who agree that God is both holy and just, it is next to impossible to find someone who will add to these elements the idea that God is wrathful.

The assumption in the world—and even in most of the church today—is that the love, mercy, and grace of God either swallow up the holiness, justice, and wrath of God or effectively trump them. It is common to hear the hymn "Amazing Grace" played or sung. But hardly anyone believes that grace is amazing. It is something we assume.

In this chapter, I want to examine a pair of biblical texts that I have preached on many times. However, I do not apologize for having made the point I wish to make before, for these are things we need to examine over and over again. The Bible says that "the LORD your God is a consuming fire" (Deut. 4:24), and we dare not forget it.

First, look with me at 1 Chronicles 13:

Then David consulted with the captains of thousands and hundreds, and with every leader. And David said to all the assembly of Israel, "If it seems good to you, and if it is of the LORD our God, let us send out to our brethren everywhere who are left in all the land of Israel, and with them to the priests and Levites who are in their cities and their common-lands, that they may gather together to us; and let us bring the ark of our God back to us, for we have not inquired at it since the days of Saul." Then all the assembly said that they would do so, for the thing was right in the eyes of all the people. So David gathered all Israel together, from Shihor in Egypt to as far as the entrance of Hamath, to bring the ark of God from Kirjath Jearim. And David and all Israel went up to Baalah, to Kirjath Jearim, which belonged to Judah, to bring up from there the ark of God the LORD, who dwells between the cherubim, where His name is proclaimed. So they carried the ark of God on a new cart from the house of Abinadab, and Uzza and Ahio drove the cart. Then David and all Israel played music before God with all their might, with singing, on harps, on stringed instruments, on tambourines, on cymbals, and with trumpets. And when they came to Chidon's threshing floor, Uzza put out his hand to hold the ark, for the oxen stumbled. Then the anger of the LORD was aroused against Uzza, and He struck him because he put his hand to the ark; and he died there before God. And David became angry because of the LORD's outbreak against Uzza; therefore that place is called Perez Uzza to this day. David was afraid of God that day, saying, "How can I bring the ark of God to me?" (vv. 1–12)

In seminary, I was taught that the biblical passages referring to sudden paroxysms of divine rage, such as the record in this passage of the killing of Uzza with no warning, manifested the truth that the Old Testament is not the inspired Word of God, but is an account of the popular religion of a semi-nomadic group of people who were pre-scientific and unsophisticated. I was taught that these episodes are totally incompatible with the New Testament portrait of the God of love revealed in Jesus. What I experienced in seminary was a revival of the Marcionite heresy, an attempt to purge from the Bible all references to the angry deity of the Old Testament.

In contrast to what I was taught, I believed that since this episode and others like it were recorded in the pages of sacred Scripture, they at least deserved to be considered with the philosophy of the second glance. I still believe that. So let us take another look at this confusing and horrifying event in the history of God's people.

An Attempt to Restore Glory

King David assembled the whole nation of Israel for this celebration. He decided to bring the ark of the covenant, the most sacred vessel of Israel's religion, to the Holy Place. After the ark had been captured by the Philistines and later returned, it had been stored away in the house of Abinadab in Kirjath Jearim, removed from the life of the people (see 1 Sam. 4–7). David wanted to restore the glory to Israel. He wanted to restore the throne of God to its proper place. So he had a new cart made to carry this precious cargo, and he had Uzza and Ahio lead the oxen that were pulling the cart carrying the ark. It was a glorious and festive occasion. The ark on its cart was accompanied by choirs singing anthems and by musicians playing harps, cymbals, and other instruments.

Then tragedy struck. This great parade was moving wonderfully until one of the oxen stumbled, and when that happened the cart tilted and the sacred ark of the covenant began to slide. Suddenly the ark was in immediate danger of falling into the dirt and mud, where it would be desecrated. Uzza, probably acting instinctively out of a sense of respect for this sacred object, stretched forth his hand to steady the ark. What does Scripture say? As soon as he steadied the ark and kept it from falling into the mud, the heavens opened and a deep voice shouted from heaven, "Thank you, Uzza!" No, that's not how it happened. As soon as Uzza touched the ark, he was stricken. God executed him instantly.

Oh, the gymnastics my Old Testament professors went through in seminary when they dealt with this passage. They would say, "That's the way it seemed to these unsophisticated Hebrews who were watching this incident, but surely the man died of a heart attack generated by his terror that he had ventured to touch the sacred object." Or my professors would say, "This is evidence that the Old Testament portrays God's wrath as arbitrary, whimsical, and capricious." One professor even spoke about the "dark side" of Yahweh, a demonic element within the nature of God Himself.

Evidently these professors never had read Numbers 4. God had designated the responsibility for the priestly duties and for teaching to the tribe of Levi. Levi was a large tribe, so it was broken down into clans, and the clans were broken down into families. One of those clans of the Levites was the Kohathites, and their sole responsibility was to look after the sacred vessels of the tabernacle, including the transportation of those vessels. If you recall, God Himself designed the ark of the covenant. It was a wooden chest covered in gold, and it had rings on the ends and in the middle. When the tabernacle was moved from place to place, the Kohathites placed lengthy poles of wood through the rings, and they lifted the ark by those poles and carried it on foot. That was God's specifically designated method for moving the ark. It was not to be carried on a cart and it was not to be touched by the Kohathites. For this reason, God said in Numbers 4:15, "They must not touch the holy things or they will die." This command was passed down from father to son to grandson among the Kohathites. Every Kohathite knew it.

We don't know for sure that Uzza and Ahio were Kohathites, but they probably were or they would not have been assigned this task. It is difficult to imagine that they did not know this command of God. Yet, when the ark began to fall, Uzza touched it.

Jonathan Edwards preached a sermon on this topic. He said that the sin of Uzza was the sin of arrogance. Arrogance? Didn't he risk his life to make sure that the ark of the covenant would not be marred or spoiled by coming into contact with the mud? Edwards said that Uzza's arrogance is seen in his assumption that contact with the mud would be a greater sacrilege than contact with the hand of a sinful human being. What is mud but earth mixed with water? There is nothing innately sinful about earth or mud. If the ark of the covenant had touched the ground, the earth would not have polluted it. But there was sin in Uzza. Contact with his flesh was far more desecrating than contact with the earth. That is why God commanded the Kohathites not to touch the ark. But Uzza arrogantly violated that command and thereby profaned the most holy object in Israel, so God executed him.

Playing with Strange Fire

We read of a similar incident in Leviticus 10: "Then Nadab and Abihu, the sons of Aaron, each took his censer and put fire in it, put incense on it, and offered profane fire before the LORD, which He had not commanded them. So fire went out from the LORD and devoured them, and they died before the LORD" (vv. 1–2). What was going on? What was the strange fire that Nadab and Abihu offered on the altar? I don't know. But whatever was in the fire that made it profane, it did not please God. These young priests were simply involved in experimental worship. Maybe they wanted to change the liturgy that God had ordained in such a way that it would be more appealing to the congregation. If so, they missed the fundamental principle of worship—our method of worship is to be determined not by what is pleasing to us but by what is pleasing to God.

The most "successful" worship service ever recorded in the Bible is found in the Old Testament. It broke all attendance records, and the singing was so full of gusto that it was heard miles away on a mountain. One of the men who heard this celebration thought a war had broken out. But when he took time to investigate, he discovered it was not a war. Instead, it was a worship service—one with a golden calf (Ex. 32). Nothing attracts greater crowds than practices of idolatry.

But Nadab and Abihu were just trying to *improve* on the worship of Israel. They devised a new way to sacrifice. They offered unique fire on the altar, and as soon as they did, fire came out from the altar and consumed them.

How did Aaron respond to this horrifying event? Let's go back a moment to the death of Uzza. According to 1 Chronicles, Uzza was killed because God was angry with him for touching the ark. When Uzza was executed by the wrath of God, who else got mad? David. Even David had trouble dealing with the wrath of God. But long before David, there was this incident in which the sons of Aaron were executed by God in His wrath. What was going on in Aaron's mind? He was a father. I can see him saying: "God, what have You done? These were my sons. They were following in my footsteps. All they did was tinker a little bit with the fire on the altar." So in obvious distress, he went and spoke to Moses. The text tells us:

And Moses said to Aaron, "This is what the LORD spoke, saying:

'By those who come near Me
I must be regarded as holy;
And before all the people
I must be glorified.'"

So Aaron held his peace. (v. 3)

The Bible is often filled with understatement, and this is one example of it. You have to read between the lines here in verse 3. Moses said: "Aaron, this is what the Lord spoke. Don't you remember what the Lord said at your ordination, when He set you apart and consecrated you to a holy vocation—that those who come near to Him must regard Him as holy?" Apparently God had given this command to the priests. But instead of regarding God as holy when they came before Him, Nadab and Abihu had come in profanity.

How often do we pastors give God equally profane worship when we dare to come into His presence without considering Him as holy, without seeing our primary responsibility in our celebration of worship as displaying the glory of God, revealing His majesty before the whole congregation? We need to think on this.

What does the text say that Aaron did when Moses gave him this reminder? Again, Moses employs masterful understatement. He writes, "So Aaron held his peace." There was nothing else for Aaron to do. There was no room for debate. God had said, "I will be regarded as holy by anyone who comes near to me."

The text goes on to say, "Moses called Mishael and Elzaphan, the sons of Uzziel the uncle of Aaron, and said to them, 'Come near, carry your brethren from before the sanctuary out of the camp'" (v. 4). Having killed Nadab and Abihu, was God now being a little bit gracious, allowing Aaron's family to recover the bodies and take them out for a proper burial? No. Moses said the bodies were to be taken "out of the camp." We are told, "So they went near and carried them by their tunics out of the camp, as Moses had said" (v. 5).

Notice what follows:

Moses said to Aaron, and Eleazar and Ithamar, his sons, "Do not uncover your heads nor tear your clothes, lest you die, and wrath come upon all the people. But let your brethren, the whole house of

Israel, bewail the burning which the LORD has kindled. You shall not go out from the door of the tabernacle of meeting, lest you die, for the anointing oil of the LORD is upon you." And they did according to the word of Moses. (vv. 6–7)

Do you see what God said through Moses? "I don't want the bodies of Nadab and Abihu in the camp. I don't want anyone rending their garments and lamenting in dust and ashes. I don't want a wake for these men. They polluted My sanctuary. I want their bodies and everything associated with them carried outside the camp, because they have profaned Me with their false worship."

Images of Divine Wrath

Perhaps the most famous sermon ever preached on American soil was preached in the eighteenth century in Enfield, Connecticut, by Jonathan Edwards. You probably know the name of that sermon: "Sinners in the Hands of an Angry God." I read that sermon for the first time in college; it was required reading as an example of sadistic preaching. I thought, even then, that a sadistic preacher would do everything in his power to tell his congregation that there was no such place as hell, while secretly enjoying the inevitability that they would plunge into it. But Edwards was no sadist. He loved God and he loved people. He cared about their ultimate destination, so he preached on the terrors of hell to encourage them to flee to Christ.

Edwards' sermon has been used in classrooms because of its graphic imagery of the wrath of God. Edwards comes under criticism for using such imagery, but the vast majority of the images he used to describe the perilous situation of impenitent people were drawn from Scripture itself. His main text, "Their foot shall slide in due time" (Deut. 32:35, KJV), draws a picture of a man crossing a deep chasm on a rope bridge that is swinging to and fro in the breeze, with planks that are covered with moss, making them slippery and hiding the ones that are rotted through, so that his every step on the bridge may be his last before he slips and falls into the abyss. Such a fall was not simply probable, it was inevitable. God warned sinners that if they did not repent, their feet would slip in time.

Another metaphor was that of a dam holding back floodwaters. Edwards said that the wrath of God is like those waters, stored up behind a dam. I remember thinking about this sermon when we were watching the televised images of the devastation wrought in New Orleans by Hurricane Katrina. The news programs showed the increasing volume of water, which posed a mounting threat to the levies around New Orleans. When one of the levies would give way, tons and tons of water would burst through and inundate parts of the city. Edwards said God's wrath is like those waters as they built up. He noted the apostle Paul's teaching in Romans 2:5: "But because of your hard and impenitent heart you are storing up wrath for yourself on the day of wrath when God's righteous judgment will be revealed." The unsuspecting person goes to bed at ease in Zion, with no fear that the dam will ever burst.

Then Edwards used the metaphor of the bow, again borrowing from Old Testament imagery. The psalmist writes, "If a man does not repent, God will whet his sword; he has bent and readied his bow" (Ps. 7:12a). It is not that God has His fingers on the bowstring and is thinking about drawing it. The bow is already bent and His arrow is aimed at the heart of the unrepentant sinner. The only thing that is keeping that arrow from flying to its target is the hand of God that holds it. But it is inevitable that if the sinner does not repent, God will release the arrow of His wrath.

Of course, the most vivid imagery in Edwards' sermon is that of the spider in the web. When Edwards was a teenager, he wrote a technical essay on the behavior of spiders, so he was knowledgeable about spiders and their webs. For example, he knew that when a heavy stone is dropped on a spider's web, the web will not hold it back; rather, the stone will burst through. In a similar way, he said, the imagined righteousness of the people would not be able to stop the fall of God's wrath.

Switching the metaphor, Edwards then compared the unrepentant sinner to a spider held over a flame. He said:

> It is nothing but [God's] hand that holds you from falling into the fire every moment. . . . You hang by a slender thread, with the flames of divine wrath flashing about it, and ready every moment to singe it, and burn it asunder; and you have no interest in any Mediator, and nothing to lay hold of to save yourself, nothing to keep off the flames of wrath, nothing of your own, nothing that you ever have done, nothing that you can do, to induce God to spare you one moment.[1]

People believe that Edwards' sermon was about wrath, and it was, but I believe it was more about the grace of God. Edwards told the Enfield congregation, "There is no other reason to be given, why you have not dropped into hell since you arose in the morning, but that God's hand has held you up."[2] Apart from the gospel, there is no reason why any of us is alive today and not in hell.

Sadly, Edwards' sermon wouldn't scare anyone in our culture or in our churches, because people do not believe in hell anymore. The most brazen lie of all is the lie people tell themselves: "I have nothing to worry about from the wrath of God. My God is a God of love." If that is your thought, your god is an idol.

An Inalienable Right to Grace?

My favorite illustration of how callous we have become with respect to the mercy, love, and grace of God comes from the second year of my teaching career, when I was given the assignment of teaching two hundred and fifty college freshman an introductory course on the Old Testament. On the first day of the class, I gave the students a syllabus and I said: "You have to write three short term papers, five pages each. The first one is due

September 30 when you come to class, the second one October 30, and the third one November 30. Make sure that you have them done by the due date, because if you don't, unless you are physically confined to the infirmary or in the hospital, or unless there is a death in the immediate family, you will get an F on that assignment. Does everybody understand that?" They all said, "Yes."

On September 30, two hundred and twenty-five of my students came in with their term papers. There were twenty-five terrified freshmen who came in trembling. They said: "Oh, Professor Sproul, we didn't budget our time properly. We haven't made the transition from high school to college the way we should have. Please don't flunk us. Please give us a few more days to get our papers finished."

I said: "OK, this once I will give you a break. I will let you have three more days to get your papers in, but don't you let that happen again."

"Oh, no, we won't let it happen again," they said. "Thank you so, so, so much."

Then came October 30. This time, two hundred students came with their term papers, but fifty students didn't have them. I asked, "Where are your papers?"

They said: "Well, you know how it is, Prof. We're having midterms, and we had all kinds of assignments for other classes. Plus, it's homecoming week. We're just running a little behind. Please give us just one more chance."

I asked: "You don't have your papers? Do you remember what I said the last time? I said, 'Don't even think about not having this one in on time.' And now, fifty of you don't have them done."

"Oh, yes," they said, "we know."

I said: "OK. I will give you three days to turn in your papers. But this is the last time I extend the due date."

Do you know what happened? They started singing spontaneously, "We love you, Prof Sproul, oh, yes, we do." I was the most popular professor on that campus.

But then came November 30. This time one hundred of them came with their term papers, but a hundred and fifty of them did not. I watched them walk in as cool and as casual as they could be. So I said, "Johnson!"

"What?" he replied.

"Do you have your paper?"

"Don't worry about it, Prof," he responded. "I'll have it for you in a couple of days."

I picked up the most dreadful object in a freshman's experience, my little black grade book. I opened it up and I asked, "Johnson, you don't have your term paper?"

He said, "No"

I said, "F," and I wrote that in the grade book. Then I asked, "Nicholson, do you have your term paper?"

"No, I don't have it."

"F. Jenkins, where is your term paper?"

"I don't have it."

"F."

Then, out of the midst of this crowd, someone shouted, "That's not fair." I turned around and asked, "Fitzgerald, was that you who said that?"

He said, "Yeah, it's not fair."

I asked, "Weren't you late with your paper last month?"

"Yeah," he responded.

"OK, Fitzgerald, I'll tell you what I'm going to do. If it's justice you want, it's justice you will get." So I changed his grade from October to an F. When I did that, there was a gasp in the room. I asked, "Who else wants justice?" I didn't get any takers.

There was a song in the musical *My Fair Lady* titled "I've Grown Accustomed to Her Face." Well, those students had grown accustomed to my grace. The first time they were late with their papers, they were amazed by grace. The second time, they were no longer surprised; they basically assumed it. By the third time, they demanded it. They had come to believe that grace was an inalienable right, an entitlement they all deserved.

I took that occasion to explain to my students: "Do you know what you did when you said, 'That's not fair'? You confused justice and grace." The minute we think that anybody owes us grace, a bell should go off in our heads to alert us that we are no longer thinking about grace, because grace, by definition, is something we don't deserve. It is something we cannot possibly deserve. We have no merit before God, only demerit. If God should ever, ever treat us justly outside of Christ, we would perish. Our feet would surely slip.

Among those now reading this book, there are many who are assuming they are not going to go to hell. But if there is a God (and there is), and if He is holy (and He is), and if He is just (and He is), He could not possibly be without wrath. If you have not been reconciled to Him through the blood of His Son, the only thing you have to look forward to is His wrath, which is a divine wrath, a furious wrath, and an eternal wrath. God must be regarded as holy by anyone who comes near Him. So if you would come into the presence of God, consider the nature of the God whom you are approaching, that you may come covered by the righteousness of Christ.

Notes

1 Jonathan Edwards, "Sinners in the Hands of an Angry God," in *Select Sermons* (Christian Classics Ethereal Library), http://www.ccel.org/ccel/edwards/sermons.sinners.html (accessed Jan. 27, 2010).

2 Ibid.

INDEX OF SCRIPTURE